To Carol

May this book take you deeper as you live this Praise

love
Phil 29/4/18

THE TRANSFORMING POWER OF PRAISE

The Key to a Life of Purpose, Freedom, and Joy

PHIL WARREN

Copyright © 2018 Phil Warren.

All rights reserved. No part of this book may be used or reproduced by any means, graphic, electronic, or mechanical, including photocopying, recording, taping or by any information storage retrieval system without the written permission of the author except in the case of brief quotations embodied in critical articles and reviews.

Scripture taken from the New King James Version®. Copyright © 1982 by Thomas Nelson. Used by permission. All rights reserved

Scripture taken from the King James Version of the Bible.

THE HOLY BIBLE, NEW INTERNATIONAL VERSION®, NIV® Copyright © 1973, 1978, 1984, 2011 by Biblica, Inc.® Used by permission. All rights reserved worldwide.

WestBow Press books may be ordered through booksellers or by contacting:

WestBow Press
A Division of Thomas Nelson & Zondervan
1663 Liberty Drive
Bloomington, IN 47403
www.westbowpress.com
1 (866) 928-1240

Because of the dynamic nature of the Internet, any web addresses or links contained in this book may have changed since publication and may no longer be valid. The views expressed in this work are solely those of the author and do not necessarily reflect the views of the publisher, and the publisher hereby disclaims any responsibility for them.

Any people depicted in stock imagery provided by Getty Images are models, and such images are being used for illustrative purposes only. Certain stock imagery © Getty Images.

ISBN: 978-1-9736-2012-9 (sc)
ISBN: 978-1-9736-2014-3 (hc)
ISBN: 978-1-9736-2013-6 (e)

Library of Congress Control Number: 2018901934

Print information available on the last page.

WestBow Press rev. date: 03/19/2018

Contents

Foreword vii
Acknowledgments xi

1. Under the Apple Tree 1
2. Created for Praise 7
3. The Realm of Praise 19
4. The Reason to Praise 32
5. The Depths of Praise 48
6. The Power of Praise 65
7. The Sacrifice of Praise 86
8. The Silence of Praise 99
9. To Live is Praise 112

Appendix 125

Foreword

Phil Warren is a man fully possessed by God. He is a man on fire, filled with the very Person, Presence and Power of Jesus Christ, exuding the love of God in such a tangible way that when you're with him, you literally *feel* that love emanating from him. I am extremely blessed that Phil is one of my best friends. Spend any amount of time with Phil and it's not long before your heart begins to burn with the contagious love for Jesus that he burns with. It's infectious!

This book is just like the author, it's infectious! As I began to read the pages, my heart started burning with God's love for me and His love for His world. Phil's incredible stories of his experiences of God's love as he's lived a life of extravagant praise has ignited the power of praise within me and given me a hunger and thirst for the living God beyond anything I've experienced before.

It's not often that I read a book that caused me to stop reading every few minutes because unstoppable praise for Jesus spontaneously erupted on my lips as the majesty of Christ, His Presence and the beauty of holiness overwhelmed me. I'm so thankful to Phil for writing this book! The Holy Spirit has used this book in a very special way to reawaken my heart to my first love, Jesus Christ our glorious King and most precious Friend forever.

My prayer for each of you, is that as you read these pages, you will experience the very presence of the resurrected King and Saviour, Jesus Christ, the God who created you and saved you in such a powerful way that spontaneous, joyful, powerful, transforming praise will be awakened in you as your heart catches fire and you will never be the same again!

This is one of those books that invite us into the opportunity to experience Jesus like the two disciples of Jesus did on the road to Emmaus. Just like those men who said, "Did not our hearts burn within us while He talked to us on the road, while He opened the scriptures," we find our hearts burning within us, reading these pages, as the same glorious, resurrected Jesus opens the scriptures to us as we join Phil 'under the apple tree.'

Its in this place we discover our very purpose! We were created for praise! Praise is the realm where deep intimate relationship with our Creator calls us out of the smallness of our lives and into the bigness of His life, far beyond the false safety of our fears and into the great adventures of His endless ocean of love.

Some of the many things that I admire in Phil, even more than his phenomenal sportsmanship and strong sense of adventure, are his humility, vulnerability and authenticity. These shine through every chapter and story in this incredible book, becoming the very context that enables us to embrace the power of praise in the depths and realities of our own struggles, failures, battles and fears, so that we like Phil, become overcomers in Christ Jesus.

Finally though, it's Phil's devotion and radical obedience to Jesus that draws us all into wanting to experience the most challenging and yet rewarding praises of all, the sacrifice of praise and the silence of praise. These chapters will set your heart on fire! May spontaneous joy well up in your heart continuously, as you embrace the invitation of Jesus into the sacrifice and silence of praise; laying your life down for the sake of Love.

To live is truly praise!

Duncan Smith
Founding Pastor, CTF Raleigh–Durham, NC
President, Catch the Fire Ministries

Acknowledgments

Writing this book on praise has in many ways been the most natural thing for me to do. Not only has this been my life's journey, discovering more of the realm, power and life of praise, and continues to be. But using the words of George Herbert, from his poem 'Praise', it is something I feel I have been set aside to do:

> Of all thy creatures both in sea and land
> Only to man thou hast make known thy ways
> And put the penne alone into his hand
> And made him Secretarie of thy praise

However in attempting this role of secretary, it is certainly not something I have tackled alone, and to that end I am extremely grateful for all the encouragement and help I have received from so many.

To friends, church family and colleagues who have inspired and championed me to write this book on 'Praise', I am enormously grateful, as I am to those who have read and edited the script, in particular Faith Allpress, Hamish Ramsay, Joseph Purnell and my wife Heather. Having parents who have both written books has been so beneficial in terms of their comments and support, and I am especially thankful to my father, Norman, for suggesting an additional chapter, the Silence of Praise.

To those who have been willing to write an acknowledgment, I thank you with deep gratitude for your kind and generous words, both written here and spoken over time, seeing the potential and calling it out. I am especially grateful to our special friends, Kate and Duncan Smith, for being part of this journey, and to Kate for inspiring the title as it stands and Duncan for introducing this work with his foreword.

But most especially my deepest thanks belong to my lovely wife Heather and our two daughters Sanna and Emily. As parents, we could not be prouder of the two of you reflecting our praising Creator and Saviour with such passion and joy, and as a husband I could not be happier to share this journey with my best friend who lives praise in such a beautiful, powerful and loving way.

With all of this said, those who know me understand the sincerity of my heart when I dedicate this book to the glory of God, and to the honour of His praise, as I continue to live His praise with purpose, freedom and joy.

Phil Warren

Under the Apple Tree

Keep me as the apple of Your eye;
Hide me under the shadow of Your wings
Psalm 17: 8 (NKJV)

PRAISE IS A beautiful and powerful essence of life. Regardless of occasion and location, its beauty and strength can be seen and enjoyed, from celebrating the first steps of a child to acknowledging the last breath of a life lived well, and this is especially so when it is directed towards God. What is fascinating about praise is not only how its effect can be outwardly observed and appreciated, but also how its realm and power can be intimately known and experienced.

I do not remember exactly when my fascination for the whole area of praise began - probably earlier than I recall - but there was certainly one memorable day that started me on this adventure. It was not so much the events that took place that marked this day out from others, but the change that happened within me.

It was the summer of 1984 and I was working as a labourer on a small river - a tributary of the River Thames - strimming the edges, removing rubbish, and stabilising the banks. On this particular day my two colleagues were further upstream pulling out the reeds and I was working alone. They had very different values and goals in life to me. I had college to look forward to in the autumn and the money I was earning was set aside for student living; they had their weekends to look forward to, and their wage packages were spent on heavy drinking. I had the privilege of knowing this fact as there was always a detailed and colourful report on the following Monday. They would recount the total consumption during their habitual Friday night brawl, evidenced by yet another missing tooth. This made it more difficult for them to divulge the information, and I wondered how long it would be before their words would be indistinguishable. Yet despite our differences, they trusted me with the tasks each day and, more importantly, with their tools to carry out the work.

The work was physical and demanding, and this stretch of the river was especially overgrown. As I waded slowly through the water, methodically strimming the banks, I found myself aching for the presence of God, and asking the Holy Spirit to come and fill me. To my surprise[1] He came! Even more to my surprise, as He came upon me powerfully, like electrical pulses, I began to break out in spontaneous praise. I remember it so clearly. I was standing under an overhanging apple tree, and the Holy Spirit's presence literally fell on me. I could not help but sing out my praise loudly, boldly, unashamedly and with utter delight, and this lasted for some time. I was in the river, filled with the Holy Spirit, praising God with all my being, singing spontaneous songs out loud and rejoicing in Him. A song rose up in me that I still remember today.

This encounter was so powerful, and yet I did not fully understand the impact it had on me at the time. I have realised since that day that a way of life had been instilled in my very being, so much so that wherever I am now praise is always in my heart and there is always

---

[1] At this point in my life, this was not a prayer I was in the habit of making. I had heard of other people being filled with the Holy Spirit, but had little expectation that this would happen to me.

a song on my lips. That moment under the apple tree, immersed in the river, changed my life and transformed my focus forever.

To allow you to appreciate what this experience meant to me, I need to give a brief précis of my life prior to that encounter. I was brought up in a loving Christian home. My parents were in full time Christian ministry in the Anglican Church. They modelled in so many ways what it is to be a faithful and fruitful disciple of Jesus[2]; and God miraculously provided for us as a family again and again. From the age of ten I attended boarding school, and in terms of my faith, I increasingly struggled with a daily form of religion that seemed to contradict the reality I knew and hungered for. Summer camps boosted my spiritual appetite, but as I neared the end of my school career I was acutely aware of a distance that I had created between God and me. I did not question His existence, but I left senior school with a deep sense of inward emptiness and harboured an unspoken dilemma: I knew God existed, but I wondered how God could love a person like me. This was about to be answered dramatically.

In September 1983, I began a gap year[3]. Initially I volunteered in a Christian retreat centre, high up in the Untersberg Mountains, overlooking Salzburg in Austria. Working alongside an ex-convict, I could see in the 'natural' that I had been blessed with so much compared to him, and yet he carried a supernatural anointing that I could only admire. We chopped wood and went for long runs in the forests together, and I came to value his wisdom. But when he returned to the UK, I was still left with a 'God-shaped hole' that needed filling.

---

[2] My father's booklet, 'Journey into life', is a wonderful expression of his evangelistic and pastoral heart, and my mother's passion for marriage counseling has helped countless relationships.

[3] It was quite common to take a year out between senior school and college/university. Both my older brother and sister had taken a gap year and it seemed the natural thing to do, especially as I really did not know what I wanted to do with my life.

One of my daily duties was to drive the children of the owners of the retreat centre down the mountain pass to attend school in the nearby village. As winter came, this task required greater time and effort. On one occasion in early December, I was carefully navigating the familiar route down the snowy mountain pass when suddenly the car hit ice as we crossed a bridge and we started to skid. We were faced with a sheer drop one side, and the rock face on the other, and as the car picked up speed, we swerved from side to side. I had lost complete control of the car and I started to panic. To this day I do not know whether I called out inwardly or outwardly for God's help, but suddenly strong arms physically came around me and took control of the steering wheel. We had been skidding for about a third of a mile, and these arms around me steered the car onto the only grassy verge on this mountain pass, where we came to a stand still. The children were unharmed. There was no scratch or damage to the car. I was deeply shocked by what had happened but somehow managed to start the car up, transport the children to school, and return to the centre to explain what had happened. Seeing how shaken I was, the owners gave me the morning off and I returned to my room and fell on the bed. On my bedside table there was a Bible that I had not yet opened, but reaching for it in that moment of desperation, the book opened at 1 John 4 and my eyes were transfixed to verse 16: *'God is love and those who live in love live in God and God lives in them'* (NIV).

It was a 'beautiful' collision. In that moment I knew God really could love a person like me, with all my mess and pain. With tears in my eyes, I knew that my 'God-shaped hole' was being filled. The Father was immersing me in His love, and I knew that in His glorious grace and goodness He had sent an angel to save me, and those with me in the car. Kneeling beside my bed, I made a renewed commitment to journey with Him and to discover more[4].

---

[4] I have since discovered that a similar thing happened to me when I was a baby. My parents were taking a youth group to Austria, and were driving down a mountain pass, when my father lost complete control of the steering. Instead

Returning from Austria for Christmas with my family, I set off in the New Year to volunteer at a retreat centre on Mount Carmel, above the city of Haifa, Israel. My heart was melting, although I knew there were still stony moments of doubt. On one occasion, a group of us had climbed up Masada[5] and we camped overnight. In the middle of the night, I took myself to the northern part of the rock, and found myself crying out to God again, shouting out into the night sky: 'If you are there, I want to know you'. Again, with the most incredible waves of love falling on me, I found myself on my knees completely immersed in His presence, breaking out in praise, overwhelmed by the wonder of His creation and the glory of His grace. It was as if heaven had enveloped me and I was joining the angels in praising the living God, surrounded by the most glorious starry display of the heavens sparkling all around me.

Another time, I was visiting Lake Galilee and I had climbed up to the Church of the Beatitudes to have some quiet time away from the group I was travelling with. This octagonal-shaped church, symbolising the eight beatitudes described in Matthew Chapter 5, is believed to be the place where Jesus gave His Sermon on the Mount. The Franciscan Sisters built it in 1938 on a low hill near Tabgha overlooking the lake. Normally this site was popular with the tourists but on this particular day, uncharacteristically, there was no one around, and so with the Galilee region spread out before me, I sat on the ground reading again Matthew's account. There was a

---

of turning around a bend, the van went straight into the forest at speed. Supernaturally the van steered through the trees to a stand still. Ordinarily it would have been impossible to navigate such a route. Aged two, I was in the back with my older brother and sister, and amazingly we were unharmed despite not being strapped in as there were no seat belts.

[5] Masada is a rock plateau on the western side of the Dead Sea, overlooking Jordan. It was formerly the Summer Palace for King Herod the Great. On the occasions we visited the rock, the Israeli army had an outpost consisting of a few Israeli soldiers, but visitors were permitted to camp overnight.

breeze rising up from the lake and I was enjoying the peace. With no noise or interruption, suddenly a lady came around the corner and stopped in front of me. Her face was glowing and she was wearing a multi-coloured dress covered with writing. As I looked closely, imprinted on her dress were the words of all the fruit of the spirit: love, joy, peace, patience, kindness, goodness, faithfulness, gentleness and self-control. She smiled at me for some time, and then disappeared. Still to this day I do not know whether she was an angel, or a visitor who loved the Lord and walked quietly. Either way, I was again caught up in the most powerful and intimate atmosphere of praise.

Many more encounters and collisions with the Holy Spirit happened to me during the year that led up to that beautiful summer's day in 1984 where under the apple tree, immersed in the river, God was calling me into His presence. He was inviting me, as He invites every person who knows they are empty and desperate for something more, to come near: *'If anyone thirsts, let him come to Me and drink. He who believes in Me, as the Scripture has said, out of His heart will flow rivers of living water'*[6]. He was drawing me into the life of praise that He has created for every living being and into the transforming power that is released when we bless Him at all times, when His praise is continuously on our lips.

My hope and desire is that as you read on you will be drawn deeper into this glorious realm and power, and you will know this reality for yourself; namely, a life of purpose, freedom and joy as we live His praise.

---

[6] John 7: 37 NKJV

Created for Praise

Let everything that has breath praise the Lord
Psalm 150: 6 (NKJV)

PRAISE IS THE outward expression of an inner delight. It is the vocal celebration of a party in the heart, however big or small, momentary or continuous[1]. When we are fed a feast that delights the palate we praise the creator for a wonderful meal. When we are given a gift that brings us joy, we praise the giver for their generosity and kindness. When we watch potential growth from a seed, we praise the producer for their effort and fruit. When we discover a new way of doing something better, we praise the revealer for their insight and wisdom. When we are captivated by the sound and sight of a performance, we praise the artist for their talent and entertainment. When we admire an act or a quality, we praise the steward for enriching life. When we see beauty displayed before our eyes, we praise the one in whom this beauty is found.

---

[1] This is the author's definition of praise. However, he recognises that there are many definitions and commentaries on praise. For example, the Concise Oxford Dictionary defines it as: express warm approbation of, commend the merits of (person, thing); glorify, extol the attributes of (God etc). Hardy and Ford, 1985, have taken this further and argued that the logic for praising is that of '…overflow, of freedom, of generosity…', and in the case of God, it is 'giving glory to Him, and enjoying Him forever' (paraphrase of the Westminster Catechism).

There is no law or requirement to this.

Praise rises up as naturally as the air we breathe, and expresses freely the delight and pleasure of one to another. Or that is how it should be; that is how we are made to be. We have been created for praise where everything that has breath is invoked to praise!

The problem arises when praise becomes a means to an end; when we praise out of duty or lip service, or use it as a way of managing situations and people for our own benefit, whether this is in the home or workplace. Jesus talks about being the 'salt of the earth' and 'having salt in you', and describes what happens when salt loses its flavour; it becomes worthless and *'good for nothing, to be thrown out and trampled underfoot by men'*[2]. In so many ways this can so easily be applied to praise. Praise is so good for our nourishment and flavours life so well, but when the outward expressions of affirmation and encouragement have little or no connection with our inner delights it very quickly loses its flavour and value to those we praise, and those from whom we receive praise.

It is interesting how in recent years scientists have started to give 'praise' more attention and significance. Whilst general words of praise were once considered beneficial, there is much more of an emphasis on both the positive and negative affects our praise can have on children and adults alike. For example, some psychologists[3] have argued that praising children for their overall ability can be harmful because it suggests that any good performance is due to natural ability, whereas poor performance is the result of natural deficiency. Commending a child for an outcome that emphasises ability can cause just as much reluctance in them to take on a new challenge - because failure signals lack of ability - as it can motivate

---

[2] Matthew 5: 13 (NKJV) and Mark 9: 50 (NKJV).

[3] There are numerous studies on this, e.g. Terri Apter, the Science of Praise (Psychology Today), posted May 26, 2009.

them to do well. Similarly adults are just as hungry for praise and yet can be volatile in their responses when it is offered. Research seems to suggest that men tend to take praise at face value whilst women reject half the praise they receive, and are more likely to analyse and evaluate it. For example, if a husband said to his wife, 'darling you are a brilliant cook', the suggestion is that she is just as likely to interpret his praise negatively – he wants to get out of doing the cooking – as she might receive it positively, as a word of thanks. The presupposition is that we have to get praise right.

Not only that, but we have to contend with the antithesis of praise, namely discouragement or lack of praise. How many of us have been crushed by a comment or shut down by a critical word? James likens this type of outward expression to a rudder that can steer a ship or a little fire that can set a forest alight, and describes the tongue as an *'unruly evil, full of deadly poison'*[4]. I still remember one senior school report and one particular word contained in it. I was not particularly interested in academic work and seemed to get by comfortably. My passion was sport and music and I succeeded in both. In addition, I was well regarded by the staff and ended up holding positions of responsibility. Of all the reports over the years that I would have received commending any successes, the only one I recall contained the words: 'He is thick'! 'Thick' is not an encouraging word of praise! At any level it implies stupidity and failure. How that could have undermined my future, further education as well as my self-worth had that word remained unchecked! I have subsequently forgiven the teacher for the comment.

We are not created for discouragement or to discourage; the heart is not fashioned for a lack of praise. Yet in learning to adapt to criticism and mask the wounds, we all too easily overlook a reality literally staring us in the face; namely we are made for praise and

---

[4] James 3: 5-8 (NKJV)

praising. I am not a scientist but I am able to understand how recent scientific work has been able to show that we are wired for affirmation and encouragement, and that when we give and receive praise there is a real, physical, electromagnetic and chemical change in the structure of our brain that brings about a positive and life-giving transformation. Rather than viewing the brain as a machine, fixed and hardwired early on in life unable to adapt and wearing out with age, as considered a few decades ago, scientists have now demonstrated through neuroplasticity research that the brain is adaptable and malleable, it has renewable characteristics, and can actually be changed by the mind[5]. We can observe and measure the activity of the mind through the firing of neurons, and know the wholesome effect praise has on the body, mind, and soul when praise is real and genuine. This is when it is an outward expression of an inner delight, and a vocal celebration of a party in the heart[6] which then benefits our whole being.

This is of course good news, but it is nothing new! Science is at last catching up with the truth that is revealed throughout the Bible that we are made in the image of the uncreated God who is worthy of all praise and yet Himself loves to praise, and has created us for praise and praising. How do we get it right then? The answer lies in His amazing grace and faithfulness, and how He has shown us the way through His Word and Spirit, as we hear His voice and receive His love. And we can see this modelled from the beginning.

In Genesis 1 we read of the history of creation: *'In the beginning God created the heavens and the earth. The earth was without form and void; and darkness was on the face of the deep. And the Spirit of God*

---

[5] It may be worth pausing at this point and reading Romans 12: 1-2 (NJKV).
[6] For further study, I would thoroughly recommend the work of Dr Caroline Leaf, in particular her book 'Switch on your brain: the key to peak happiness, thinking and health' Published by Baker Books, 2013.

was hovering over the face of the waters'[7]. God, Father, Son and Holy Spirit, was on the move[8]. We know from John 1 and Colossians 1 that this was a perfectly united and beautifully worked outward expression of the Trinity, in whom and by whom all things are made. As for the time scale of creation, whether it happened over a six-day period, in stages, or over billions of years, important though it is, that is not for discussion here. In a perfect relationship of oneness and all-togetherness, God reveals a truth and reality about Himself here that is also found elsewhere in the pages of the Bible; namely He loves to praise. His very being breathes out and speaks out praise, and we can see this taking place right at the start of creation.

We know there are many mysteries and secrets about God that are unattainable to us, and Paul reminds us in 1 Corinthian 13 that what we know now is known in part. But what we find here is one revelation about God that most certainly belongs to us and to our children forever[9].

Six times in this opening chapter we read the words: 'God saw that it was good'.

> When He saw the light, He saw that it was good (vs. 4);
> When He saw the waters under the heavens gathered together into one place, and the dry land appear, He saw that it was good (vs. 10);
> When He saw the earth bring forth grass, herbs that yield seed according to its kind, and trees yielding fruit, He saw that it was good (vs. 12);

---

[7] Genesis 1: 1-2 (NKJV)
[8] The Hebrew word for God, *Elohim*, though the form is a grammatical plural, the meaning is singular implying the co-equality and oneness of the Trinity.
[9] Deuteronomy 29: 29 (NKJV)

> When He saw the two great lights, one to rule over the day and the other over the night, as well as the stars, He saw that it was good (vs. 18);
> When He saw the sea creatures and birds of the air, He saw that it was good (vs. 21);
> When He saw the beasts of the earth, the cattle and everything that creeps, He saw that it was good (vs. 25)[10].

God looked upon His creation with inner delight. The Hebrew word for 'saw', *ra'ah*, means to see, literally or figuratively, with numerous applications such as to look upon another with approval, to gaze with enjoyment, and to find delight. There was a vocal and outspoken celebration of the holiest of parties where together the Father, Son and Holy Spirit praised each part of creation for its goodness. *Towb*, good, has the widest sense of meaning, drawing out the best and the most beautiful, the sweetest and that which brings the most pleasure. As each 'day' was completed, God was gazing with enjoyment as the absolute goodness and beauty of His creation was unfolding before His eyes, and in response praised each stage as it came into being: you are good. Day after day as He found delight in the herbs and fruit trees, sea creatures and birds, the sun and moon, and the beasts of the earth, He praised creation with the declaration: you are good! You are good! You are good!

If this was not enough, His praise poured out even more on the sixth day, as He made man in His image, according to His likeness: '...*in the image of God He created Him; male and female He created them*' (vs. 27, NKJV). Seeing everything He had made, He celebrated with the declaration of absolute praise: you are very good.

The English word 'very' is used so often in spoken and written language that we have come to understand it as implying the next

---

[10] Genesis 1 ((NKJV)

level up. A very good film is better than a good film, but there is always room for improvement. A very good wine is better than a good wine, but it is not the best. A very good marriage is preferable to a good marriage, but the marriage would not necessarily be considered perfect; and so on. However, *M'od* (the Hebrew word for 'very' in this passage) implies something quite different. If *M'od* was on a scale between one and ten, it would imply ten if not higher; if *M'od* were quantified, it would be the difference between the ceiling and the sky. As a word it implies the superlative (the very best), and refers to that which is exceedingly great, mighty and perfect. In other words, God offered the very best praise over His creation when He saw that it was very good. His praise was not lacking in any way; there was no sense of duty or lip service in His voice. His delight over us was unconditional and immeasurable; it was off the scale. His vocal celebration perfectly reflected the joyful party in His heart as time and eternity met together and life was formed.

Let everything that has breath praise!

What we see in the first book of the Bible is the Father, Son and Holy Spirit exemplifying what it is to praise. This opening chapter unveils a revelation of who God is, and how He loves to praise and bless His creation, and especially *'man made in His image ... blessed to be fruitful and multiply, to fill the earth and subdue it; to have dominion over the fish of the sea, over the birds of the air, and over every living thing that moves on the earth'*[11].

When my two daughters were born there was such inner delight and enjoyment as I held them in my arms and gazed deep into their eyes, but there was no way this party in my heart could remain silent. For both girls, born three years apart, I took four large pieces of plywood and painted on them, in large white lettering, 'our baby is born!

---

[11] Genesis 1: 27-28 (NKJV)

Thank you Jesus' and placed it outside our house for everyone in the neighbourhood to see. I rang up my family and friends to tell them the good news. I ran into the staffroom to inform my colleagues[12]. I even shouted it out to my first class of the morning: 'I have just had a new baby! I am just so excited!' They certainly joined in the celebration, cheering and congratulating me; although I'm sure they were equally delighted to delay the start of the lesson!

When God saw the birth of His creation, He was full of praise. When He delighted in the perfection of all He made, He was full of praise. When He gazed at man made in His own image, He was full of praise; and His praise was of the highest degree for the ones He loved. Knowing Him, as I am learning to more and more, I can imagine His outspoken celebration echoed all around the universe itself for the relationship with us that He had been longing for and looking forward to enjoying. Maybe Revelation 4 gives us insight into how His praise over creation was received in the throne room of heaven; *'You are worthy, O Lord, to receive glory, honour and power; for You created all things, and by Your will they exist and were created'*[13]. Whether this is the case or not, His delight in celebrating over us has continued ever since.

In the Old Testament, we see Him praising Abel for his excellent sacrifice (Genesis 4: 4), and Noah for being a just man, perfect in his generations, walking with Him (Genesis 6: 9). He praises Abraham for his faith and *'accounted it to Him for righteousness'* (Genesis 15: 6, NKJV), and Moses for His humility, for being very humble, more that all men who were on the face of the earth (Numbers 12: 3). He praises David for having a heart after His own heart (1 Samuel 13: 14; Acts 13: 22), and Solomon for his desire for wisdom (1 Kings 3: 10). In the Psalms we see Him delighting in us, as we delight in Him (Psalm 37: 4), and having precious thoughts towards us, so much so that as we hear them spoken over us, we discover they are simply too many to

---

[12] I was a senior school teacher at the time.
[13] Revelation 4: 11 (NKJV)

count (Psalm 139: 17-18). Psalm 149, in particular, gives us a wonderful picture of the Lord celebrating over us: *'For the Lord takes pleasure in His people; He will beautify the humble with salvation'* (verse 4, NKJV). If we were to amplify the verse, drawing out the full meaning contained in the Hebrew text, it would read something like this: 'For the Lord sets his affection towards His people, full of approval and enjoyment, taking delight and pleasure in them; He will embellish, beautify and boast over those who humble themselves before Him with health, deliverance and salvation'. In fact, there is a further meaning to the word 'beautify', which is to shake a tree. What a glorious visual of the Father's praise, shaking the tree of salvation over us, so that we can taste and enjoy its fruit; the fruit of the Spirit[14] in the presence of His delight.

Then there is the well known and often cited passage in Zephaniah 3, where we discover that God rejoices over us with His love and singing: *'The Lord your God in your midst, the Mighty One, will save. He will rejoice over you with gladness, He will quiet you with His love. He will rejoice over you with singing'* (3: 17, NKJV). The latter phrase, 'rejoice over you with singing', is all about making a joyful noise, celebrating over us with an explosion of sound and singing. How He rejoices over us with His delight, as a parent to a child; and it is not only when life is going well.

Following the loss of a loved one, when Sarah and John McMillan wrote the song 'He loves us' they captured so well the heart of the Father and His delight over us, even in times of hardship and pain:

> So we are His portion and He is our prize
> Drawn to redemption by the grace in His eyes
> If grace were an ocean we're all sinking
> So heaven meets earth like a sloppy wet kiss
> And my heart turns violently inside of my chest

---

[14] See Galatians 5: 22-23 (NKJV)

> I don't have time to maintain these regrets
> When I think about the way He loves us[15].

We see this revelation of our praising God in the New Testament as well. When Jesus was baptised by John, and came out of the water with the Spirit descending like a dove and alighting on Him, the Father audibly praises His son: *'This is my beloved Son, in whom I am well pleased'* (Matthew 3: 17, NKJV). When the seventy returned from the mission field with joy, Jesus praises the Father: *'I thank you Father, Lord of heaven and earth, that you have hidden these things from the wise and prudent and revealed them to babes'* (Luke 10: 21, NKJV). When the disciples rebuked those who were bringing children to Jesus for Him to touch, Jesus takes them up into His arms and blesses them. *Eulogeo*, the Greek word for bless, is to speak well of, to thank and to praise.

Our creator God, Father, Son and Holy Spirit, is a God who loves to praise His creation, and in particular His children, because He loves His creation. The wonder of it all is that we are made in His image, which means we too are created for praise: to give and receive praise as He does. Inherent in our very nature and being is the foundation for us to be those who, like Him, outwardly express our inner delight. As the Psalmist writes: *'Out of the mouth of babes and nursing infants, you have ordained praise'*[16]; it is who we are and who we have been created to be.

But there is a convergence to this praise. Whereas God's praise is directed towards us, His creation and all those who are made in His image; our praise should be directed towards Him, our creator, the One who has made us in His image. In other words, there is a pinnacle of fulfilment and expression from which all our praise flows; and that is, first and foremost, that the very substance of our praise is

---
[15] John and Sarah McMillan, CCLI 5032549, 2005 Integrity's Hosanna! Music.
[16] Psalm 8: 2 (NKJV)

founded and grounded in God. He is our praise and He is our God[17]. There is no substitute for this in praising another or get out clause to such praise of Him; there are no exceptions or replacements. The mistake society has made over the years and throughout history is centering praise on idols and people in preference to our creator God. Praise must wholly and eternally be focussed on Him.

Psalm 150 brings us back to the reality of who we are in God: '*let everything that has breath praise the Lord*' (verse 6, NKJV). This is not just a call for us to lift up our praise to the Lord, important though it is to respond to such an invitation; neither is it a suggestion on a Sabbath day or Sunday morning to make a loud noise to Him with whatever instrument we have in our possession, as fun as that would be. It is a declaration of who we are and a command to be who we are made to be. So that when we praise, we perfect in us that which has already been made perfect in His image; when we praise, we complete in us that which has already been made complete in Him; when we praise, we breathe as we are meant to breathe; when we praise, we move into the fullness of the life He has ordained for us; when we praise we dwell in His presence as He dwells with us, because our God of praise loves to inhabit the praises of His people, as we will see in the next chapter.

~

Personal response

1. Read Psalm 100, slowly and meditatively, allowing the Holy Spirit to reveal more of who you are, made in His image, and created for praise.
2. In Proverbs 8: 3, as we remove the layers, we have a picture of the Spirit of Wisdom, the Holy Spirit, pursuing us with

---

[17] Deuteronomy 10: 21 (NKJV). Also Jeremiah 17: 14 (NKJV).

His voice, calling out by the gates and at the entrance of all the doors to our lives. Take time out to listen to God's voice speaking and singing over you, and write down what you hear.

Decree over your life:

I command my spirit to attention and my mind and body to come in line with my spirit, and I decree: I will awake from everything that holds me back, and arise to be the child of praise God has created me to be.

The Realm of Praise

But thou art holy. Thou inhabitest the praises of Israel
Psalm 22: 3 (KJV)

OVER THE YEARS I have visited a number of impressive buildings in many different nations, from cathedrals and churches, galleries and opera houses, palaces and parliaments, biblical landmarks and world-renowned sites. It is not that I have intentionally sought them out; it has just happened.

Some time ago I took a school trip of forty teenagers to Venice and Rome, and along with the adventures of being burgled, attacked and the nation undergoing a national strike, we were able to enjoy the delights of the Piazza San Marco and Grand Canal in Venice, and the inspiring Coliseum and St Peter's Basilica in Rome. Heather and I are not particularly drawn to seek out buildings of architectural importance on days out, but on occasions we have taken day trips to London, and have enjoyed visiting landmarks such as the National Art Gallery and Buckingham Palace. More recently, on a stopover trip to New York, we were so grateful to be able take the lift to the observatory at the top of the Empire State Building to witness first-hand the incredible view over the city. It was quite breath-taking, seeing with a bird's eye view the Statue of Liberty, the Hudson River, Manhattan and Central park, and then watching night time fall over a myriad of lights.

As a family we have visited Paris, amongst other places, and loved the time we spent at the Eiffel Tower, Le Louvre, and Nostradamus Cathedral, which our daughters then likened to a Disney ride. We could understand their confusion as we had just come from Disney Land Paris, and admittedly when we first entered into the darkened entrance, it could easily have been mistaken for the Pirates of the Caribbean ride. The Amity Bible Press, in Nanjing (China) was a remarkable building, not so much for its design but for its functionality, and the way its clockwork precision utilised both labour and space brilliantly, resulting in the production of so many bibles (at the time they were nearing one hundred and thirty million copies). Then, of course, I have also visited the many famous sites and edifices in Israel, rich in biblical and political history, such as the Church of the Holy Sepulchre and the Temple Mount. I have even been locked up in one of these buildings, in Lazarus' tomb, along with my brother, whilst the guard went off for his twenty-minute lunch break, not realising that two visitors were inside in complete darkness. Or maybe he did!

But for each building and site of special interest that I have visited, whilst I can admire the stunning architecture, the skilled craftsmanship, the story behind its creation and its subsequent history (knowing that with greater knowledge there would be more to admire and marvel at), there is a common denominator which actually applies to every building and edifice ever made: namely, without life in them or the presence of someone, they are empty vessels. These buildings need to be lived in, dwelt among, inhabited and enjoyed for them to fulfil their purpose as structures of greatness.

There is a principle at work here that can be applied to the whole realm of praise; namely what we build in terms of our structures of praise only has life if God is living in the building; what we construct in terms of our forms of praising only has breath if God is permeating the constructing; and what we offer in terms of our sacrifice of praise only has fullness if God is present in the offering. For centuries we have built churches and places of worship for us to inhabit in order to praise God, and many people have courageously dedicated their life's work to building for the glory of God. But since the beginning of our divine relationship, God has chosen to inhabit our praises in order for us to dwell with and in Him, and for Him to build His church through us[1]. Psalm 22: 3 reveals a wonderful truth about His preference for us when it comes to our praise. In His very nature of holiness His primary desire is to make His home in the outward expressions of our inner delights; namely our praise:

> '*But thou art holy. Thou inhabitest the praises of Israel*' (KJV).

The Hebrew word, *Yashab*, means to remain, settle, abide, inhabit, sit down, and to make your home. There is no hint of the transient or temporary. There is no sense of restriction, such as parking your vehicle in the short-term parking bay for a limited amount of time. This word means to dwell with the intent to stay. Our holy God longs to abide and remain in the praises of His people.

Yashab also means to enthrone: '*But you are holy, enthroned in the praises of Israel*' (NKJV, AV), which captures so well not only His Kingship – that He alone is Lord and He sits on the throne of our lives – but also His kingdom; the domain in which He rules and reigns. This is the realm of praise where He loves to be.

In this revelation, God is affirming His preference is not to inhabit a building in order to receive our praises. His primary desire is to inhabit our praises so that we can come in and inhabit Him; where His praise over us blends and energises our praise to Him. This is

---

[1] I use the word 'church' here in its generic sense, referring to God's people as the body of Christ.

of critical importance when it comes to our understanding of praise and its power.

In this context, one of the most tragic incidences in the Old Testament is when Moses and the people are at the foot of Mount Sinai. In Exodus 19: 17, we read how Moses brings the people out of the camp to meet with God, and that Mount Sinai is completely covered in smoke because *'the Lord descended upon it in fire. Its smoke ascended like the smoke of the furnace, and the whole mountain quaked greatly'* (NKJV). This is a momentous occasion in the life of the Israelites.

Previously they had witnessed the great deliverance from Egypt, the parting of the sea, the manna from heaven, the water from the rock, and the victory over the Amalekites. They had experienced His awesome power and their praise testified to His glorious triumph: *'The Lord is my strength and song, and has become my salvation. He is my God and I will praise Him'*[2]. Three months have passed since the Exodus, and here they are in the wilderness of Sinai consecrating themselves before the Lord to meet with Him[3]; to encounter His fiery presence, and to discover His heart for them. And yet, the tragedy is that this did not happen. Why not?

Let me first give some context to this in the form of a personal testimony. In 2008 I first experienced the fiery presence of the Lord. We had taken a group of leaders from our church to Toronto Airport Christian Fellowship (as it was known then[4]), and prior to going my prayer was to know more of the power of God. I had heard people

---

[2] Exodus 15: 2 (NKJV)

[3] *Qir'ah,* to meet, means also to encounter and to seek.

[4] The church is now called Catch the Fire Toronto, and Heather and I will be forever indebted to John and Carol Arnott and the wonderful ministry teams they have lead over the years for steering so faithfully the values that mark them out and have changed our lives: knowing the **F**ather heart of God;

speak about catching the fire, and could see the manifestations of this in their lives, but it was not something I had encountered myself and I was so hungry for 'more of God'. The Leaders and Pastors conference we attended was inspiring, but by the end of the conference, although I had loved the freedom in the worship and the teaching, and had taken every opportunity for ministry, I had not experienced the 'fire of God' that I had hoped for. Our flight home was not until later on the Sunday evening, and so we were able to stay for their Sunday service. I thought: Lord, maybe this is the time! But again as much as I enjoyed the sweetness of the Holy Spirit's presence, I had nothing to write home about.

At the end of the service, I was admittedly a little disappointed. I repented of any wrong attitude, released my prayer to the Lord, asked for his peace, and settled in my spirit that it was not meant to be. As we were saying our goodbyes to Duncan and Kate Smith at the front of church[5], Duncan spoke to us about the 'fire', and in his passionate and compassionate manner decreed 'fire' over us both. With that Heather and I simultaneously flew backwards under the power of God, and for myself I stayed at the front of church on the floor for the next three hours as the Holy Spirit's supernatural fire enveloped me and grew with increasing waves of intensity. After a while Heather and the group went back to the hotel to check out, and one member stayed by my side as I groaned outwardly with every pulse of His power, and burned more intensely as I was caught up in this beautiful and yet awesome encounter of His presence. At one point, children were kicking a ball over me as the team from the Spanish Church were getting ready for their afternoon service. I was fully conscious and yet pinned to the floor. It was only when I cried out to God knowing my body could not take any more of His holy fire and I thought I would literally die, that the intensity

---

intimacy with Jesus; restoring the foundations of our lives through healing; and empowerment in the Holy Spirit; and, of course, having fun.
[5] At the time, Duncan was Executive Director of the church

started to lessen, and I was able to be helped to my feet and stagger back to the others. For two days, I was still shaking from this furnace experience. The glory of His fire landed on me and I was forever changed. I discovered in a new and fresh way the Father's heart for me as I pursued Him with all my heart, and tasted something of His power. To be honest, I was grateful I survived.

What I experienced then, and countless of others have experienced throughout history, is the inward fire of God. Returning to our Israelites, at the foot of Mount Sinai, they were being invited to meet with God and to encounter not only His fiery presence inwardly, but to experience it visibly and outwardly and to discover His heart for them.

> *'As the Lord says to Moses, who in turn shared these words with the people: 'I bore you on eagles' wings and brought you to Myself. Now therefore, if you will indeed obey My voice and keep my covenant, then you shall be a special treasure to Me above all people; for all the earth is Mine. And you shall be to Me a kingdom of priests and a holy nation*[6].

They were not so much as standing under an apple tree, but under the most glorious and awesome fire cloud. To the Lord, they were His jewels in the crown, and they were about to be invited into the inner most realm of His praise.

> God's audible voice[7] was the outward expression of His inner delight to establish a special relationship

---

[6] Exodus 19: 4-6 (NKJV). For further insight, *bow'* the word for 'brought' means to abide, carry, fetch as well as bring in; *cgullah* means valued property, treasured possession.

[7] C.f. verse 9: 'And the Lord said to Moses, "Behold, I come to you in the thick cloud, that the people may hear when I speak to you, and believe

with this group of people whom He saw as a Holy Nation; His desire was to inhabit this priceless possession and their praise, as a kingdom of priests.

And the people's response altogether was to say 'yes' to the entire word that the Lord had spoken to them.

In obedience to the instructions they were given, the people then washed their clothes, purified themselves inside and out, so that they would be ready to meet with God on the third day. They knew they had to get this right, or else there would be serious repercussions[8]. And so, on the third day, it came to pass[9].

With thundering and lightning, the sound of loud trumpets, thick smoke on the quaking mountain blazing like a furnace, God descended in the fire of His presence to meet with Moses and the people and to speak to them. He gave them the Ten Commandments and invited them to meet with Him. This was a new day for His kingdom of priests and holy nation; a dayspring of drawing near as God's own special children. But instead of faith rising up in them, what we see in verses 18 and 19 is fear taking its hold on them. The people were afraid of God's presence and so they 'stood far off', despite Moses' encouragement to come close. In those few days their response had changed from a resounding 'yes' to a trembling 'no', and they made the choice to stay away.

As Moses commented to them, in the next verse, this was a test to see their hearts: *'Do not fear for God has come to test you and that*

---

forever". So Moses told the words of the people to the Lord' (NKJV). God had even made it easier for the people to believe; they could audibly hear His every word to Moses.

[8] Exodus Chapter 19: 11-24 (NKJV)

[9] It is interesting to note that in God's kingdom, the third day signifies release, freedom, resurrection and new life.

His fear [holy reverence] *may be before you, so you may not sin* [miss out]' (NKJV). *Nacah*, to test, means also to prove something or to adventure. God wanted to see how intentional they were about meeting and enjoying this adventure with Him. He wanted to test their hearts to see whether, like Moses (and Joshua), they would pursue His presence above all things. However, the sad and tragic reality was that this holy nation kept at a distance from their holy God and in doing so missed out on the realm of praise that belonged to them; His presence and the beauty of His holiness. Moses, on the other hand, spoke with the Lord face to face as a man speaks to His friend[10], and shone with the glory of the Lord so much so that he had to wear a veil to speak to the people, so bright was the skin of His face[11]. And Joshua, his servant, did not depart from the tabernacle; he stayed in the very place the Lord chose to inhabit[12].

Herein lies a perpetual challenge to us. When it comes to the presence of God, where are we positioning ourselves? Near or far? When it comes to the realm of praise, who or what is doing the inhabiting? In His faithfulness and love God honours His word and allows us to have the desires of our hearts, even when these desires are rooted in our own ideas and responses of what this inhabitation should look like. A poignant example of this is the original vision for a temple in Jerusalem.

In 2 Samuel 7, we read at the start of the chapter that David was now dwelling in his newly built palace and that *'the Lord had given him rest from all his enemies around him'* (vs. 1, NKJV). In other words - and reading between the lines - he had time on his hands for a new project. With undoubtedly honourable motives, he looks out one day and sees the Ark of the Covenant housed in a tent, compared to the splendour of his palace, and formulates a plan to build a house

---

[10] Exodus 33: 11 (NKJV)
[11] Exodus 34: 29-35 (NKJV)
[12] Exodus 33: 11 (NKJV)

for the Lord fitting for His presence. He shares the idea with the prophet Nathan, his friend and confidant, who consents to the idea and encourages David to do *'all that is in [his] heart, for the Lord is with [him]'* (vs. 3, NKJV). That night Nathan is corrected by God in a vision, and goes to David in the morning as the mouthpiece of the Lord with a prophetic revision. Firstly, God does not need a temple or building to dwell in, and Israel's history has born testimony to the effectiveness of His choice to move about in a tent (vs. 6-7). Secondly, who does David think he is to build a house for God? It is God who is building the 'house' for David, and the 'house' He is building is the unique and special covenant relationship with him and His people that will be established forever (vs. 8-17)[13].

Commenting on this passage, Eugene Peterson puts it like this: 'There are times when our grand human plans to do something for God are seen, after a night of prayer, to be a huge human distraction from what God is doing for us. That is what Nathan realised that night: God showed Nathan that David's building plans for God would interfere with God's building plans for David'[14].

Nonetheless David's vision became a reality, with the baton being picked up by his son Solomon, and the temple was built. On the very mount where God told Abraham to sacrifice his son Isaac (Genesis 22: 2), and a thousand years later the very threshing floor that David purchased from Araunah the Jebusite in order to offer a sacrifice for his sin in ordering a census (2 Samuel 24: 18-25), Solomon began

---

[13] In this word to David, given through Nathan, it is interesting to note how God-centric this message is. God is the first-person subject of twenty-three verbs and each of these verbs carry the action. Contrary to David's perception of this great work he is going to undertake for God, God is reminding him comprehensively of what He has done, is doing and is going to do, which will far exceed anything David can imagine.

[14] Eugene H. Peterson, Leap Over a Wall: Earthly Spirituality for Everyday Christians, p.160, Harper, 1997.

to build the first temple on Mount Moriah in 966 BC (1 Kings 6: 1-2; 2 Chronicles 3: 1). After seven years, he completed the work (1 Kings 6: 38), and the temple then stood for three hundred and eighty years before the Babylonians under King Nebuchadnezzar tore it down in 586BC. The exiled Jews then returned to their land after seventy years, having been given permission by Cyrus the Great to rebuild the Temple. In comparison to Solomon's magnificent edifice, the structure Zerubbabel erected seemed modest. However, it was improved by the Jews following the first Maccabean triumph, and then received its greatest make-over when Herod the Great began a massive reconstruction and renovation in 20BC that continued for the next eighty-three years. This was the temple Jesus taught in, whose destruction he predicted in Matthew 24. This was the meeting place for the early church who were there continuously praising and blessing God (Luke 24: 53), and the likely location when they were filled with the Holy Spirit at Pentecost (Acts 2). However, in AD70, Titus sent in his Roman legions who reduced the temple to rubble; in a few days they destroyed what had taken decades to construct. Jesus was right: *'Not one stone shall be left here upon another, that shall not be thrown down'*[15].

On an ordinary piece of land, that was once a threshing floor, an extraordinary building was constructed, twice, to honour the Lord, and twice destroyed. It began with one man's dream, as Solomon testifies at its dedication: *'Now it was in the heart of my father David to build a temple for the name of the Lord God of Israel'*[16]. It continued with others capturing the vision, but it came to a sudden end. Why? This was not God's idea, and anything that is man made cannot and does not last.

What happened to God inhabiting the praises of His people during those terrible periods in history when buildings were destroyed and

---

[15] Matthew 24: 2 (NKJV)
[16] 2 Chronicles 6: 7 (NKJV)

lives were lost? Nothing! There was nothing gained and nothing lost. Why? Because God is not dependent upon physical buildings to meet with us. There was and is no change to how He chooses to meet with us, even when the storms are raging. There was and is no amendment to the place in which He loves to inhabit, namely our praises, even in the midst of pain! As from the beginning, until now and always, God is searching for hearts that are open to Him. He is seeking that holy space He has created in each of us, made in His image, so that He can come and abide as we lift up our celebrations to Him. His preference is always to inhabit our praise over and above anything we build or construct even if it is for His name and for His glory.

If only we would grasp the depths of this truth, the body of Christ, the church, would look very different to the world and be very different in the world.

God's desire for His people is so much bigger than anything we can build. His heart for His children is so much more than all we can ever imagine or dream.

Jesus revealed this to the Samaritan woman in John 4: *'Woman, believe me, the hour is coming when you will neither on this mountain or in Jerusalem, worship the Father … the hour is coming, and now is, when the true worshippers will worship the Father in spirit and truth, for the Father is seeking such to worship Him'*[17]. The reality is that even if He voiced the idea to David to build a home for Himself, there would be nothing David or Solomon (or us for that matter) could have built that would ever be big or strong enough to contain His presence.

Stephen draws this out when he is standing before the Sanhedrin, prior to his martyrdom: '… *the most High does not dwell in temples*

---

[17] John 4: 21-23 (NKJV)

made with hands, as the prophet says, "Heaven is my throne and the earth my footstool. What house will you build for Me? Says the Lord, or what is the place of my rest? Has not my hand made all these things?" You stiff-necked and uncircumcised in your heart and ears! You always resist the Holy Spirit; as your fathers did, so do you"[18].

Our creating, praising God has chosen above everything else to dwell with us, His people, as we outwardly express our delight in Him; and we need to know that anything less than this misses out on the fullness and richness of all He has for us.

Recently, one of our young adults came to faith. He attended an Alpha course we were running, and had such a powerful experience of the Holy Spirit during one of the sessions that the next day he came to church for the first time. Prior to this, as far as he could remember, he had never been to church. He had no Christian grounding or upbringing, which also meant he had no 'baggage' when it came to church itself. By his own admission, the music he listened to was poles apart from anything he heard in church, and he even had a poster on his bedroom wall that said 'he hated God'. As we began to praise God with singing, I turned around to see him standing on the side, gazing around with his mouth wide open; no noise was coming out, yet that expression remained for the rest of the service. Afterwards, I raced up to him to ask him how he found his first experience of church. Knowing he liked music, I questioned him first about the songs. He said this: 'normally I would have found the music irritating. But because God's presence was here, I loved it'.

The wonder of His love and mercy is that God has turned everything upside down and inside out. Rather than desiring the outward things we have made, He directs His gaze to the inside, to the hearts that

---

[18] Acts 7: 48-51 (NKJV). Stephen is citing Isaiah 66: 1-2 (NKJV).

are drawn and open to Him, inviting us to meet with Him so that He can come and inhabit our praise.

This is the realm of praise.

To stay away out of fear, or to stand at a distance, is to miss out! To think we know best and imagine we can contain Him with our ideas is to lose out. He is worthy of all our praise, and as we will discover in the next chapter, is wholly the reason for our praise.

Personal response

1. Read Psalm 95 a few times, and then read it again out loud, but this time make it personal; for example: *'I will come, I will sing to you Lord. I will shout joyfully to the Rock of my salvation…'* (NKJV).
2. Ask the Holy Spirit to show you any areas of your life where you are standing at a distance from God out of fear, or preventing Him from inhabiting your praise because you are too contained or reserved in your praise. Repent, and begin to praise Him freely.

Decree over your life:

I command my spirit to attention and my mind and body to come in line with my spirit, and I decree: I choose to be an open vessel for the Holy Spirit for Him to come and inhabit, as I praise Him.

The Reason to Praise

For God is the King of all the earth;
Sing praises with understanding
Psalm 47: 7 (NKJV)

I LOVE ALL sport! I always have! Though the days of competitive team sports are reluctantly over for me, I still enjoy the involvement and challenges, whether it is sea swimming, cycling, skiing, tennis, or even croquet on our front lawn. I also take great pleasure in watching certain sports, such as Rugby Union, with a preference to seeing a game live when the opportunity arises. What intrigues me, nearly as much as the game itself, are the supporters who attend these games. A few years back, I went with my family to watch the Premiership Rugby Union final at Twickenham Stadium (London) and prior to the game, I could not help but overhear the conversation of two men seated in the row behind me. In short, they were pouring out their 'woes' to each other in terms of marriage, work and health and I was close to turning around to offer them ministry when the teams ran out onto the pitch and their whole countenance changed. Caught up in the excitement of 80,000 fans, these two men were now captivated by the celebration of sport. They were delighting in their team, rejoicing in their success, although when it came to the referee not every outward expression towards him would be considered 'praiseworthy'. It was a remarkable transformation. They had a reason to praise.

The truth is, of course, such a scenario can be found anywhere in the world. Whether it is American football in the USA, cricket in India, or wrestling in Mongolia, there is an atmosphere of praise and praising that captures those who attend or watch such an event, and regardless of the tests and tribulations of life, in that moment they find reason for praising those who they consider are praiseworthy.

In the light of this global phenomenon, what has happened then to our praise of God?

If a natural human inclination wherever we are on this planet is to attend an event that we know will last just a short moment of time, and find reason enough to praise another with utter abandonment and delight, it is reasonable to question what has happened to the praise of our creating, saving God, Father, Son and Holy Spirit, who is eternal, unchanging and always worthy of praise[1]. The answer must be simply this: we have lost sight of the reason.

Again and again in scripture we read of how creation praises its Creator. In Psalm 148: 3, the sun, moon and stars are encouraged to praise God, along with the rest of creation. It is important to note that this is not figurative language, but an outward expression of a present reality that science has helped us see more clearly. Since the scientific principles discovered by Sir Isaac Newton, a new science has developed ways in showing how the vibrations on the sun's surface can be measured as the surface of the sun moves. In other words, scientists have found that the sun actually rings like a bell; and not only that, but that it rings over so many frequencies that there are several million resonances going on all at the same time:

---

[1] I am reminded of a wonderful book by A.W. Tozer, 'whatever happened to worship', in which he writes: 'men and women on this earth ought never to fool themselves about the reality of true worship that must always be in spirit and truth. It is plainly possible to have religious experience and forms of worship that are not at all acceptable to God', p.32-33, OM Publishing, 1985.

> '*Praise Him, sun and moon; praise Him, all you stars of light*' (NKJV).

The word for praise, *halal*, in its primitive root, has to do with sound and clarity, noise and light. Remarkable! The Sun truly is making a beautiful and glorious sound to the Lord[2]! In Psalms 19: 1-4, we have another revelation of this magnificent reality: '*the heavens declare (caphar) the glory of God; and the firmament shows its handiwork. Day unto day utters speech, and night unto night reveals knowledge. There is no speech nor language where their voice is not heard. Their line [sound] has gone out through all the earth, and their words to the end of the world*' (NKJV). In the skies as well as on earth and in the seas, there is the audible 'declaration' and ringing sound of praise to God and for His glory, from creation towards the Creator, in every place where speech and language is heard, and beyond. *Caphar* means to declare, tell out, and to celebrate. It literally means to score with a mark. Here we have creation recording its praise of God, day after day, and night after night; and again, science has the tools to pick up the sounds[3].

One of the most well-known and cited passages for nature's praise comes in Isaiah 55: 12: '*For you shall go out with joy, and be led out with peace; the mountains and the hills shall break forth into singing before you, and all the trees of the field shall clap their hands*' (NKJV). Far from interpreting this passage as a metaphor for 'human praise' (because it characterises human actions), what the prophet is sensing and seeing is the voluminous sound of creation rising up to the One who has made it all, and who sustains all things by His love and power. Isaiah perceives the 'breaking forth[4]' in loud celebration of

---

[2] Scientists have long known that the earth does a similar thing, and that the moon has its own 'song' too.

[3] It is worth taking a break at this point, and listening to Louie Giglio's 'Mashup of Stars and Whales singing God's praise' on YouTube.

[4] Breaking forth, *patsach*, means making a loud and joyful noise

God's word being accomplished as creation is restored and redeemed by His grace; ultimately this is achieved in the coming of Jesus Christ. As Jesus himself said, even if there is no praise coming from the mouths of his followers, the stones themselves will cry out[5].

In other words, in these and other passages[6] there is a relationship between creation and its Creator that resounds with praise both outwardly and upwardly, naturally and supernaturally; and it is more than creation praising God by simply being itself; nature has reason to praise.

Theology cannot explain this adequately, and neither can science define it completely. Both disciplines draw out details and offer some answers that are undoubtedly helpful and instructive. But with the language of faith and a renewed mind for the King and His kingdom, we are moved beyond the 'why' and 'how' to the mystery that this is what it is and always will be[7], until the point of Christ's second coming, when there will be a new heaven and earth. The great theologian Karl Barth rounds this off so eloquently when he writes: 'when man accepts again his destiny in Jesus Christ... he is only like a late-comer slipping shamefacedly into creation's choir in heaven and earth, which has never ceased its praise[8]'.

What then has happened to this late-comer? Why do we see throughout history man slipping in and out of creation's choir, losing voice and sight of the One who is forever worthy of all our praise?

Undoubtedly a substantial element to answering this question lies in the whole matter of free will. Innate in our very nature and existence

---

[5] Luke 19: 40 (NKJV)
[6] For example, Psalm 66: 4 (NKJV) and Isaiah 44: 23 (NKJV).
[7] The Bible tells us that all of creation, everything, is held together in Jesus, Colossians 1: 15-20 (NKJV).
[8] Karl Barth, Church Dogmatics, p.648

is the God-given freedom to choose; to choose how we behave and to whom our praises are directed, and we have always made effective use of this gift, whether for good or bad. In terms of deities and the divine, over the years we have on the one hand created so many 'gods' within our monotheistic and polytheistic belief systems that it is not surprising cultures are confused, people groups are misplaced in their affections, and individuals are ignorant when it comes to the one true God. In fact, we see in every era and epoch an inseparable link between religion and society, and an interwoven thread of the effects and devastation caused by these man-made ideals based on freewill. The Bible has its own story to tell in this respect, of how God's chosen people have not been immune from 'slipping away' on account of free will. Notable among the many examples in Scripture is the poignant moment when the Israelites fall into the idolatry of making a golden calf out of their own earrings with the intention of worshipping it and offering sacrifice[9]. What this and other instances highlight is simply the ease in which we slip away from the One we are created to praise and fall into the trap of directing our celebration to that which we have imagined or created. How we have gone to extraordinary lengths to do this in our pursuit of what theologians call the 'numinous experience'[10]!

But then, over the years, we have also created ideals and philosophies that have undermined and denied any such reason to praise a deity

---

[9] Exodus 33. It is significant that the 'golden calf' incident takes place soon after the awesomeness of God's fiery presence resting on Mount Sinai, and His desire to meet with the people and establish a special covenant relationship with them, along with all the miraculous signs and wonders that had brought them to this point.

[10] 'Numinous' is an English adjective, derived from the Latin word numen, meaning a 'spirit or deity presiding over a thing or space'; hence the phrase the 'wholly other'. It is a word made popular by Rudolf Otto in his influential work, Das Heilige, 1917, in analyzing religious experience. [*The Idea of the Holy*. Trans. John W. Harvey. Oxford: Oxford University Press, 1923; 2nd ed., 1950].

or the divine. Defined in many different ways, but rooted in a spirit of 'atheism', such an expression of the freewill has been in existence at least as long as the records themselves[11]. Though proportionately small in terms of the numbers of adherents, there have been times in history when this free will approach has received considerable attention, and certainly in the West today, 'atheists' are still making a vociferous noise. Few could have imagined, including Nietzsche himself, the way his 'God is dead' theology would have been used and misused by those who succeeded him[12].

The point with all this is that we have freely turned our gaze to 'another' or have knowingly silenced the God-given voice that has been wonderfully tuned within us since the beginning of our creation. Either way, all too often we have lost the voice of praise for the One who is *'great and greatly to be praised'*[13].

---

[11] Historical records of atheist philosophy span several millennia. For example, in early Indian thought, there are records of atheistic schools in existence during the Vedic period, c. 1750 to 500 BC. In terms of Western atheism, it had its roots in Greek philosophy, but did not emerge as a distinct world-view until late Enlightenment, 18th Century.

[12] Friedrich Nietzsche (1844-1900) wrote this infamous statement 'God is dead' a number of times throughout his works. The meaning of the phrase is often misunderstood, whereby many have interpreted as him believing in a literal death or end of God. Instead, the line points to the western world's reliance on religion as a moral compass and source of meaning. Nietzsche's works express a fear that the decline of religion, the rise of atheism, and the absence of a higher moral authority would plunge the world into chaos. The western world had depended on the rule of God for thousands of years — it gave order to society and meaning to life. Without it, Nietzsche writes, society will move into an age of *nihilism*. Although Nietzsche may have been considered a nihilist by definition, he was critical of it and warned that accepting nihilism would be dangerous.

[13] Psalm 48: 1 (NKJV), Psalm 145: 3 (NKJV), and 1 Chronicles 16: 25 (NKJV)

But then there is another related element to the answer why we keep slipping in and out of creation's choir which is foundational: and that is to do with our 'fallen-ness' or what we term 'sin'. As Paul writes in Romans 3: 23: *'All have sinned and fall short of the glory of God'*[14]. There is a double emphasis in this verse both on us 'missing the mark', and in doing so not sharing in the prize, but also of us 'falling short' of God's glory, and in this state of falling, lacking what is requisite in drawing near to Him. And this, as Paul writes, applies to all humanity – all means everyone who has and ever will live.

Here in this passage and later on in the letter to the Romans, Paul is presenting a train of thought that identifies not only the state we find ourselves in before God, but the original source of this 'sin' and God's response and answer: *'For as by one man's disobedience many were made sinners, so also by one Man's obedience many will be made righteous ... But where sin abounded, grace abounded much more, so that as sin reigned in death, even so grace might reign through righteousness to eternal life through Jesus Christ our Lord'*[15].

Theologians have developed this teaching in what has become known as the 'doctrine of original sin' (also called ancestral sin), and over the years they have characterised the concept in different ways[16]. However, in terms of Paul's teaching, two matters are clear: firstly, as a result of the rebellion in Eden, Adam's sin has affected the nature of the whole of the human race[17] and consequentially we

---

[14] 'Sin' in the Greek, *hamartano*, means to err, offend, or trespass, but its literal meaning is to 'miss the mark'.

[15] Romans 5: 19–21 (NKJV). C.f. Psalm 51: 5 (NKJV)

[16] For example, Irenaeus, the 2nd century Bishop of Lyons, was the first to develop this doctrine. He believed that Adam's sin had grave consequences for humanity, that it was the source of human sinfulness, mortality and enslavement to sin, and that all human beings participated in his sin and shared his guilt.

[17] In Genesis 3, we read of both Eve and Adam being tempted to eat the fruit of the tree of Knowledge of good and evil, and as a consequence of disobeying

all fall short of God's glory. Secondly, in view of His great mercy, God has provided the only redemptive solution possible, which is found in the person of Jesus Christ: *'For as by Adam all die, even so in Christ all shall be made alive'*[18]. It was because of God's great mercy that cherubim were placed to guard the tree of life in the garden so we would not be removed forever from His presence[19]; and it was because of His great mercy, that Jesus came to redeem once and for all that which is lost so that we could be restored to His presence for eternity.

> *'But God who is rich in mercy, because of His great love with which He loves us, even when we were dead in trespasses, made us alive together with Christ (by grace you have been saved), and raised us up together, and made us sit together in the heavenly places in Christ Jesus, that in the ages to come He might show the exceeding kindness toward us in Christ Jesus.*
> *For by grace you have been saved though faith, and that not of yourselves, it is a gift of God, not of works lest anyone should boast.*
> *For we are His workmanship created in Christ Jesus for good works, which God prepared beforehand that we should walk in them'.*
> (Ephesians 2: 4-10, NKJV)

In other words, without Jesus we continually fall short of offering the praise we are created to bring; without His saving grace, we continually 'miss the mark' in terms of who He is, and the honour that is due to His name; and without a true and living faith in Jesus, we lose sight of the reason for our praise, and freely turn to 'another'

God's instruction, being driven out of the Garden. They were the first to experience the effects of 'missing the mark' and 'falling short'.
[18] 1 Corinthians 15: 22 (NKJV)
[19] Genesis 3: 24 (NKJV)

or silence the God-given 'voice'. However, the good news is that with Jesus and in Him we can just as easily slip back into creation's choir in heaven and on earth, with shame wiped away, and sing His praises with understanding, knowing God is the King of all the earth[20].

This is so beautifully illustrated when Jesus encounters the Samaritan woman at the well, and, finding her 'voice' again, she unashamedly tells her kinsmen: *'Come, see a Man, who told me all things that I ever did. Could this be the Christ?'*[21]. Her eyes were opened to the reason for praise.

By definition, 'reason' as a noun is to do with a cause, explanation, or justification for an action or an event; it is also to do with the power of the mind to think, understand and form judgments rationally and logically. As a verb, it means to think, understand, and form judgments with logic and rationale. In Psalm 47, the sons of Korah are encouraging the people to *'sing praises (zamar) with understanding (sakal)'* (NKJV). This literally means to chant or make music as an act of praise, with our intelligence, skill and wisdom; in other words, praising with the mind as well as with the body and heart. This is inherently significant both with respect to our thoughts and judgments towards the God we praise, but also our explanations and justifications for what we do as we outwardly express our praise corporately and in private.

'Understanding' the One to whom our praise is directed has a two-fold prong. On the one hand, it involves understanding 'who God is not', namely He is not just another deity to be worshipped and adored. On the other hand, it involves understanding 'who God is'; that He alone is the One true God, and there is no one like Him in all of heaven and earth.

---

[20] Psalm 47: 7 (NKJV)
[21] John 4: 29 (NKJV)

The former needs only a brief explanation, as the very nature of 'who God is' more than adequately deals with the question of negation. However, in a culture that loves to compare, and a society that favours tolerance over truth, relativism over absolutism, it is important at the very least that we alert ourselves to the potential dangers of comparison; namely comparing theistic beliefs. For instance, a common feature in the pursuit of inter faith dialogue is to find the lowest common denominator, so that relationships can be established. Whilst this is beneficial at one level, it has also the unwelcome affect of reducing or minimalizing truth. The God of our Lord Jesus Christ cannot be likened to another deity, along with the millions of others worshipped today. His character cannot be reflected in the structures and buildings erected in His name. His presence cannot be limited to a dedicated space of adoration; and His appearance on earth cannot be compared to that of other renowned religious leaders or prophets. Such comparisons simply take us down the path of misplaced and misleading judgments of 'who God is not'.

Jesus draws attention to this kind of misunderstanding when the Samaritan woman says to Him: *'Our fathers worshipped on this mountain, and you Jews say that in Jerusalem is the place where one ought to worship'*. Jesus has to gently remind her that God is not restricted to a location, and neither is His character reflected in the structures that have been built. He is not like the 'god' they imagine they are worshipping, as He corrects the woman: *'You worship what you do not know'*. This is not 'who God is'. Jesus is clear in this revelation: *'God is Spirit, and those who worship Him must worship in spirit and truth'*[22].

Herein lies the glorious truth of 'who God is': namely, our Creator and Redeemer God is the Lord of Lords and King of Kings. He has no equal. He is not another 'god'. He is unique from every other being

---

[22] Verse cited from John 4, in this paragraph, are: verse 20, 22 and 24 (NKJV)

because He alone is infinite and uncreated. He is above all things and before all things, and in Him all things hold together[23]. He has no beginning and no end[24]. He is immortal and omniscient. He is not limited in power or conditional in His love. He is not reserved in His grace, or restricted in His peace. He is not lacking in authority or absent in His ruling. As the Psalmist cries out: *'who is like the Lord our God?'*[25] It is of course a rhetorical question that does not require an answer, except the answer has already been given in the previous verse: *'The Lord is high above all nations, His glory above the heavens'*.

Who is like our God?

Michael, one of the seven archangels in Hebrew tradition and the only one identified as an archangel in the Bible[26], bears this very question in his name: Miyka'el means 'who is like our God' (Latin, Quis ut Deus), implying there is no one like God. The angel who leads the Lord's heavenly armies reflects the nature of the Lord in his very being. And the Lord Himself declares this question: *'To whom then will you liken Me, or to whom shall I be equal', says the Holy One'*[27]. The unequivocal answer that reverberates throughout all of Scripture is: *'Therefore You are great, O Lord God. For there is none like You, nor is there any God besides You'*[28].

The Bible is instructive in that we are made in the image or likeness of God[29]. But it is equally direct in its message that this does not

---

[23] Colossians 1: 16-17 (NKJV)

[24] Revelation 21: 6 (NKJV), and Psalm 90:2: 'Before the mountains were brought forth, or ever You had formed the earth and the world, even from everlasting to everlasting, You are God' (NKJV).

[25] Psalm 113: 5 (NKJV)

[26] Jude 1: 9 (NKJV)

[27] Isaiah 40: 25 (NKJV)

[28] 2 Samuel 7: 22 (NKJV); c.f. Exodus 8: 10 (NKJV)

[29] Genesis 1: 27 (NKJV)

mean we are equal to Him and can be compared to Him, when it comes to His sovereignty and power. There is none like Him.

Even the name He gives to Moses at the burning bush reveals His infinite uniqueness. Rather than compare Himself to another created being, or liken Himself to something Moses could relate to, He proclaims His name, and in doing so identifies Himself as One who is entirely and altogether set apart from any being or any thing:

> *And God said to Moses, 'I AM WHO I AM.'*
> *And He said, "Thus you shall say to the children of Israel,*
> *'I AM has sent me to you.*[30]

This insight into His sovereignty was something about which David learnt to be wise when he sings with understanding: *'What is man that you are mindful of him, and the son of man that you visit him'*[31]. In a similar way, the prophet Jeremiah gives prominence to this when he decrees: *'There is none like You, O Lord. You are great, and Your name is great in might'*[32].

We are reminded in Deuteronomy 29: 29 that *'the secret things belong to the Lord our God, but those things which are revealed belong to us and to our children forever, that we may do all the words of this law'* (NKJV). There is absolute mystery and wonder about God that is beyond our knowing. But throughout the Old and New Testaments, and through every personal and shared encounter with Him, God reveals to us His nature and character; and not only is this something that wonderfully belongs to us and our children, but it is a revelation that grows with every word, touch and gift from heaven.

---

[30] Exodus 3: 14 (NKJV)
[31] Psalm 8: 4 (NKJV)
[32] Jeremiah 10: 9 (NKJV)

He is the God of wonders, who shows His wonders in the heavens above and signs on the earth beneath (Acts 2: 19, NKJV). He is the God of eternity, who is from everlasting to everlasting (Psalm 90: 2, NKJV). He is the Spirit of knowledge and understanding (Isaiah 11: 20, NKJV), and the God of incomparable beauty (1 Chronicles 16: 29, NKJV). He is the giver of revelation (1 Corinthians 2: 10, NKJV) and the King of glory (Psalm 24: 8, NKJV). He is the Lord who is great and greatly to be praised (1 Chronicles 16: 25, NKJV), and the God who is our refuge and strength (Psalm 46: 1, NKJV). He is the God of love (1 John 4: 16, NKJV), mercy (Jeremiah 3: 12, NKJV), and grace (1 Peter 5: 10, NKJV).

He is Jehovah Rapha our healer (Exodus 15: 26, NKJV) and Jehovah Jirah our provider (Genesis 22: 14, NKJV). He is Elohim Kedoshim, the Holy God (Joshua 24: 19, NKJV), and He is Elohim Chaiyim, the living God (Jeremiah 10: 10, NKJV). He is the God who restores our souls (Psalm 23: 3, NKJV), and the God of peace (Hebrews 13: 20, NKJV). He is the God of our salvation (Psalm 18: 46, NKJV), and the God of forgiveness (Nehemiah 9: 17, NKJV). He is Elohay Tehilati, the God of My Praise (Psalm 109: 1, NKJV).

He is Abba Father, whom Jesus reveals (Mark 14: 36, NKJV), and the Saviour to all (John 3: 16, NKJV)[33]. He is the Spirit of truth (John 16: 13, NKJV), and the One through whom streams of living water will flow out of our hearts (John 7: 38, NKJV). He is the

---

[33] In A.D. 451 a council of Christian bishops at Chalcedon summed up centuries of debates about the person of Jesus Christ. It affirmed Him as '… perfect in Godhead and perfect in manhood, truly God and truly man … to be acknowledged in two natures, inconfusedly, unchangeably, indivisibly, inseparably; the distinction of natures being by no means taken away by the union, but rather the property of each nature being preserved, and concurring in one Person and one Subsistence, not parted or divided into two persons, but one and the same Son, and only begotten God, the Word, the Lord Jesus Christ'. This has become the classic definition.

bread of life and the light of the world. He is the gate and the good shepherd. He is the resurrection and the life. He is the way, the truth and the life. He is the true vine, in whom we can abide and bear much fruit[34]. He is the same yesterday, today and forever (Hebrews 13: 8, NKJV). He is the Lord our God, whom we are invoked to love with all our heart, soul, mind, and strength[35]. Above everyone and everything, He is the reason for our praise and our praising.

There is of course so much more to write. With every statement and title scribed here, there are a myriad of other ways to express who God is, and an ocean of truths to expound. With every comma there is a pause to wonder at His character, and with every completed sentence, there is another to extol His nature. Where would this end? The answer is simple: there is no epilogue in finding cause, explanation or justification for our praise. We can so easily identify with the words of John at the end of his gospel, when he concludes: *'I suppose that even the world itself could not contain the books that would be written. Amen'*[36]. This is certainly true here.

No amount of books will ever be able to contain our reasons for praising the Father, Son and Holy Spirit.

The logic will continue forever and a day.

There will always be further knowledge about His creative powers and uncreated nature. There will always be deeper thoughts about His saving grace and redeeming love, and how He has delivered us from the '… *powers of darkness and conveyed us into the kingdom of the Son of His love, in whom we have redemption through His blood, the*

---

[34] The seven 'I am' sayings of Jesus in John's gospel: 6: 35; 8: 12; 10: 9; 10: 11; 11: 25; 14: 6; 15: 1 (NKJV)
[35] Mark 12: 29-30 (NKJV)
[36] John 21: 25 (NKJV)

forgiveness of sins[37]. In the forming and reforming of our judgments, there will always be newer ways of rationalising His name and His nature. And in terms of joining creation's choir in heaven and earth, there will always be greater understanding in singing about the One who is worthy to '*receive glory and honour and power*'[38].

> We have an infinite and limitless reason to praise our Lord God who is deserving of all praise. Why would we settle for anything less?

Critics might conclude that this is what the church has done down the ages: we have contained and controlled the atmosphere of praise, reduced it to a liturgical style or formulaic structure, and settled for mediocrity. In many establishments, this would be difficult to deny. With ample ammunition, they could quite rightly say the methods and styles we adopt when the 'ecclesia' comes together are too formal, too reserved, too familiar and too dry! Any truth to such a commentary would not reflect the God of our praise. It is not His character that would be called into question, but ours.

We have a choice that is based on our freewill and freedom to find reason moment by moment to praise God. We have an invitation with every intake of air and utterance we voice to declare His glory. There is never a millisecond of life when we cannot explore at least a thousand aspects of His character that are worthy of honour.

> The reasons to praise God far outweigh the time we have to do so.

God has created us wonderfully and mysteriously in His image not only to be those who innately praise, but to be those who, redeemed by His love, instinctively praise Him the God of love. If, as we have

---

[37] Colossians 1: 13-14 (NKJV)
[38] Revelation 4: 11 (NKJV)

seen, our natural human inclination is to attend a momentary event and find reason enough to praise another with utter abandonment and delight, whatever is going on in our lives, how much more should our God-given proclivity be to praise Him in everything and in every way. How much more should our time and energy be given to attend the eternal event, joining in with creation's choir, and find reason to sing praises with understanding, knowing God is the King of all the earth.

Personal response

1. Reflect on the names and titles of God. Read the scriptures, meditate on them and outwardly start to praise Him with understanding, delighting in who He is, and who you are to Him.
2. Ask the Holy Spirit to show you where you have knowingly or unknowingly become too formal, too reserved, too familiar and too dry in your offering of praise. Be honest with Him and with yourself. Repent, and begin to praise Him freely.

Decree over your life:

I command my spirit to attention and my mind and body to come in line with my spirit, and I decree: I choose to live out my identity and discover afresh each day the reason for singing praise with understanding, holding nothing back, pursuing the very best, and offering all to God who is King of all the earth.

The Depths of Praise

Deep calls unto deep at the noise of your waterfalls;
all your waves and billows have gone over me.
The Lord will command His loving kindness in the daytime
and in the night His song shall be with me
Psalm 42: 7-8 (KJV)

IN SEPTEMBER 2010 I agreed to take on a five-mile swim. As a family we are very involved in the Kenyan Children's Project and, at the time, the charity needed to raise funds to support our work with street children in Kakamega, Western Kenya. In order to emphasise the plight of the children we were rescuing, we launched a fund-raising challenge with the distinct aim of attempting something that would take a person out of their comfort zone both in terms of familiarity and difficulty. For me, running, walking and cycling were activities that I loved to do, and still are, so anything that involved distance on foot or on a bike was not an option. As we live on an island, the next and most obvious choice was to attempt something in the sea. Unfortunately, there was little doubt as to what would cause me the greatest challenge; and that was swimming! I was fine in a pool, but swimming in the sea out of my depth was another matter.

On our many trips to Kenya we saw the dreadful and distressing conditions these street children had to endure; in truth it was a miracle how so many survived. I knew that anything I attempted bore little comparison to their reality. However, sea swimming for me was as hard as it could get. Not only did I have to contend with the temperature and distance, but I also had to deal with fear: the fear of being out of my depth, and what was lurking beneath me. This was especially true in the first few weeks of training. Time and time again, the theme tune to the film 'Jaws' would ring in my ears (without exaggeration), and I would be literally gripped with palpable fear, often when I was furthest from shore. The only way I could carry on was to do deliverance prayers[1] on myself and sing songs of praise; not the easiest thing to do when your face is mostly in water. However, as time went on, the fear dissipated and I came to enjoy and relish my time in the water, and on 25th September I was able, along with a friend, to complete the five-mile sea challenge.

The reason for mentioning this is that I discovered something beautiful and new in the process. Up until that point, my limited experience of swimming was contained between the four walls of a pool, and involved going up and down a lane, generally covering a similar number of lengths with the same freestyle stroke. There were times when I might look out to sea, especially when the conditions were glassy calm, and have that momentary desire to swim out into the deep. But generally, any time I spent in the sea was either on a surfboard or kayak, or in the shallows by the shore, and my preference was always swimming in a pool. All this changed when I committed myself to the deep.

As my body adapted to the temperature, and as I grew to enjoy and respect being out of my depth, I found a freedom and a space that is simply not possible in a pool. I could swim in any direction. I was not confined by walls or inhibited in my stroke. There was so much space. I could swim faster, or just soak and float. I could dive down

---

[1] This involved confessing the fear, repenting of it, and commanding it to leave me (a basic form of Restoring the Foundation Ministry prayer), whilst in the water.

deeper, or tread water. I came alive in the water, and the more I swam, the more I wanted to swim. There was a complete renewal of my heart, mind, body and soul towards swimming in the sea, and it is still there today. I find pools restrictive and restraining. I love the freedom and the space.

I believe there is a powerful analogy here in terms of praise and the depths we are prepared to go in our praising.

> Our praise was never intended to be contained within four walls.

Our offering of praise was never meant to have a shallow end to it, where we can stand secure on our own two feet; neither was it designed to have a deep end that actually has little depth, and does not get deeper. We have not been created by our praising Creator to be a people of restraint or restriction, going up and down 'stroking' God with the same familiar style. Why would we ever imagine this to be the case[2]?

The deep is calling! God longs for us to know the freedom and space He has created, as the 'deep in Him calls to the deep in us'. He wants us to go deeper in our praise, as His 'waves and billows go over us'. It thrills Him when we choose to go out of our depth, and allow His beautiful and awesome song to be sung over us as we bring our praise to Him in the daytime and at night[3]. But this requires the kind of

---

[2] It is important to note that this comment is not aimed at any one tradition, denomination or movement. As much as a high liturgical format can be contained and restrictive, so can a charismatic approach of worship, word and ministry go though the motions without depth or freedom. I have witnessed both.

[3] Deep calls unto deep at the noise of your waterfalls; all your waves and billows have gone over me. The Lord will command His loving kindness in the daytime and in the night His song shall be with me (KJV). Psalm 42: 7-8.

commitment and passion needed to enter the sea; an unreserved, uncontained, even undignified immersion into the deep.

In truth, we will know the evidence of this kind of commitment in us simply by reflecting on our own responses to those times when a praising community immerses itself into such freedom and space. Our judgments speak for themselves. We will certainly know the extent of this kind of passion simply by observing the manner in which we praise the God of glory in the secret place. Our attitudes have their own voice. The problem arises when sooner or later we can no longer keep this to ourselves. A striking example of this is found in 2 Samuel Chapter 6.

King David is now reigning over all of Israel, as well as Judah. The threat of his enemy, the Philistines, is diminishing with every conquest, and at this point they have been driven back as far as Gezar[4]. We are told in 1 Chronicles 14: 17, that the '*fame of David went out into all lands, and the Lord brought the fear of him upon all nations*' (NKJV). There was political stability and now was a good time not only to establish Jerusalem as the centre of administration, but also as the focal point of worship, and so David decided to arrange for the Ark of the Covenant to be brought to the city.

> '*So they set the ark of God on a new cart, and brought it out of the house of Abinadab ... and David and all the house of Israel played music before the Lord on all kinds of instruments of fir wood, on harps, on stringed instruments, on tambourines, on sistrums and on cymbals*'[5].

---

[4] 2 Samuel 5: 17-25 (NKJV). Gezer is on the edge of Philistine plain, some 24 miles from Jerusalem.
[5] 2 Samuel 6: 4-5 (NKJV)

This was a loud and exuberant offering of praise. This was breaking out of the liturgical walls of containment and splashing unreserved into the deep[6]. But what followed was not in David's script. When they arrived in the neighbourhood of the capital, Nachan's threshing floor[7], in the midst of their celebration, the oxen stumbled and Uzzah (who was accompanying the cart) reached out and took hold of the ark, presumably to steady it. However, his action incited the anger of the Lord against him, and whether the ark crushed him or he was divinely struck down, the passage is clear to state that *'God struck him there for his error; and he died there by the ark of God'*[8]. Not surprisingly, his death threw a dark cloud over the whole joyous occasion and brought a complete stop to the procession; and under David's direction, the ark remained in that area at the house of Obed-Edom the Gittite.

Reflecting on the incident, one might be tempted to question the severity of Uzzah's fate in relation to the seemingly light nature of his offense. However, a closer examination of the text raises two significant issues about the depths of our praise. The first is to do with how the ark, the presence of God, was carried. Setting the ark on a 'new cart' was in fact a hasty and careless decision, and whether David instructed this or inadvertently allowed this to take place, he was violating the express command of God how to carry the ark; namely to use poles made of acacia wood overlaid with gold[9]. He was negligent in how the presence of God was to be carried, taking for granted the depths that he was entering into, and this proved to be an important and painful lesson for him to learn. The deep

---

[6] Along with thirty thousand choice men of Israel, from Baale Judah (2 Samuel 6: 1-2, NKJV).

[7] Or Chidon's (1 Ch 13: 9, NKJV). The Chaldee version renders the words, "came to the place prepared for the reception of the ark," that is, near the city of David (2 Sa 6: 13, NKJV).

[8] 2 Samuel 6:7 (NKJV)

[9] See Exodus 25:10-22 (NKJV)

cannot be taken for granted just as swimming in the sea cannot be approached without care.

The second issue is to do with Uzzah's response when the oxen stumbled. The evidence suggests he was a Levite, and if not, he would have certainly been well instructed in the law. He would have undoubtedly known that it was forbidden to touch the ark (Numbers 4: 15, 19-20), upon pain of death, and whether his familiarity was the root of his actions or not, God saw the presumption and irreverence in his heart and he paid the ultimate price. Familiarity, even with that which is most sacred, is apt to breed contempt.

This is a good moment to press the 'pause' button. I have been a pastor for a number of years, and sadly one of the common denominators I have noticed (spreading across denominations, traditions, communities and nations) is the ease and speed in which a haphazard approach to God's presence becomes the norm. Or to express this slightly differently, how easily and quickly we move from passion to presumptuous familiarity in how we praise God, and settle for this preferred option, when the Holy Spirit is continually inviting us to go deeper. Does this matter? I believe it does, and Scripture strongly suggests this is the case[10]. It matters whether we are more concerned about how dignified and important we look, rather than how God sees the state of our hearts and what we are bringing to Him; and as David discovered, large numbers and impressive sounds are not necessarily the key. Being masters of familiarity, contained and reserved in our praising, is not God's will or the way into His depths. Whatever our style, expression or even

---

[10] One example of this is Psalm 40: 3-10, when David declares: 'Praise to our God ... sacrifice and offering you did not desire ... I delight to do your will, O my God, and your law is within my heart ... Indeed I do not restrain my lips, O Lord your yourself know ...' (NKJV).

personality type[11], the deep calls to the deep, and the approach we take matters to God.

Three months made all the difference for David. Whether he was more shaken by Uzzah's death or his own carelessness, he dealt with his fear[12] and dived into the deep again; this time with an attitude of obedience and care, and a heart desperate to know more of God's presence. There was nothing familiar about this praise party.

> *'And so it was, when those bearing the ark of the Lord had gone six paces, that he sacrificed oxen and fatted sheep. Then David danced before the Lord with all his might; and David was wearing a linen ephod'*[13].

This was total abandonment in praise, unreserved thanksgiving, and uncontained singing and shouting to the Lord. Not only had David laid down any kind of dignity in what he was wearing[14], but he also let go of any reservation. He danced with all his might, *ōz*, which means with boldness, exerting great force and strength; he shouted, *truw'ah*, like trumpet blasts, making a loud noise to the Lord; he 'leaped' and 'whirled' before the Lord, using all his body, right until the ark came into the city and was set in place in the midst of the tabernacle that he had erected for it. Unashamedly he committed everything in this offering of praise, and chose to give his whole

---

[11] There is not the space to discuss 'personality types', except to say whether we see ourselves as an introvert or extrovert, a responder or contemplator, God has created us all uniquely for the 'deep' of His love and presence. What prevents us from going deeper in our praise is not down to our 'type' but our heart's response.

[12] 2 Samuel 6: 9 (NKJV)

[13] 2 Samuel 6: 13-14 (NKJV)

[14] The linen ephod was the simple clothing of a priest, cf. 1 Samuel 2: 18 (NKJV) and 1 Chronicles 15: 25-27 (NKJV). Laying aside his royal robes, David was identifying with being a humble priest, just as God called Israel to be a Kingdom of priests (Exodus 19: 6, NKJV).

heart, mind and body, and there was no holding back. And when he had finished offering all the burnt and peace offerings to the Lord, he blessed the people 'in the name of the Lord of hosts', gave them gifts, and returned to bless his own household[15].

It is at this point that God reveals to David the contrast between the poolside and the sea shore; the difference between being too familiar and reserved in our praising, compared to diving into the freedom and depths that He longs for us to know and enjoy. Michal, David's wife and daughter of Saul, looked at her husband *'... leaping and whirling before the Lord; and she despised him in her heart'*[16]. Later on, her judgments and attitude are voiced to David: *'How glorious was the king of Israel today, uncovering himself today in the eyes of the maids of his servants, as one of the base fellows shamelessly uncovers himself'* (NKJV). She looked and she despised; she saw with eyes of restraint and spoke with words of contempt; and in doing so, missed out on the blessing that was hers also to enjoy.

Despising someone in their freedom or showing contempt towards them when they long to go deeper was not just a condition of the past; sadly, it still happens today. However, it is a very dangerous place to be in, and this is especially true for church pastors and leaders; it simply leaves us barren and dry, and actually alone. This is what happened to Michal. Her intention was to bring shame and embarrassment to David. Her goal was to shut down this freedom and contain his passion. She thought her 'despising' would cause him to fear what the people thought of him as King. How often does this still happen today in our meetings and services? How often do we fear what others think of us, especially those like Michal who have mastered the look of 'disdain' when freedom is in the room? But as David reveals, there is nothing for us to fear. Refusing to be controlled, he responded by telling her that the very opposite would

---

[15] 2 Samuel 6: 17-20 (NKJV).
[16] 2 Samuel 6: 16 (NKJV).

happen; namely, he would continue to play music before the Lord, and would be even more undignified and humble, and would be held in honour for doing so[17]. He could discern her spirit of restraint and because his spirit was crying out for more of God's presence, the outcome also meant that he kept his distance from her from that day on. David had fully committed himself to the deep!

This kind of praising involves the whole body.

This kind of commitment into the deep involves everything we are and all that we offer; nothing less. If it is less, then may I gently suggest that such attitudes and actions need challenging? The Father, Son and Holy Spirit are worthy of so much more, and the Lord longs for us to discover greater depths.

So what holds us back from being unreserved in His presence? What keeps us poolside, in the safety of familiarity? What draws us to prefer containment in our praise, rather than seek the freedom of the deep?

Part of the answer seems to revolve around our language, and the way we speak about praise. When we declare a thing, as the Scriptures say, it will be established for us, and light will shine on our ways[18]. If we place limits and boundaries around our understanding, we are establishing a way of being, and over the years I believe this is what many have done with 'praise'.

Without wanting to fall into generalisations, we have a tendency to draw distinctions for example between praise and worship; and this in itself can have a restraining order. It is often said: praise is about God and worship is to God. Praise is opening up and worship is entering in. Praise is about declaring and worship is about

---

[17] 2 Samuel 6: 20-22 (NKJV)
[18] Job 22: 28 (NKJV)

bowing down. Praise is celebrating what God has done and worship is adoring who He is, and so on. There are even those who would claim that praise correlates to singing loudly to more upbeat songs, clapping and dancing, celebrating and giving thanks, whilst worship is associated with falling to our knees, singing softly, bowing down, and being lost in awe and wonder. Whilst there are examples in scripture and in our experiences to confirm each of these individual descriptions, as a whole such an emphatic definition merely limits the depths of praise as it does the breadth of worship[19]. Clearly worship, by its very definition[20], means to give worth to something or someone, and in respect of God, praise naturally seems to be a subset of a larger set we call worship. However, we praise God not only for what He has done, but we praise Him for who He is. We praise Him not only with shouts of joy, but we praise Him when we are cast down and disquieted[21]. True praise is rooted in deep worship, just as in the depths of worship we bring our heart-felt praise to God. And the very words we find in both the Hebrew and Greek texts reflect this powerfully. There are many examples, but let me outline a few.

One of the most frequently used words for praise in the Old Testament is *halal* (where we get the word 'hallelujah[22]'). Found in numerous passages such as the opening verses of Psalms 146, 147, 148, 149 and 150, it means in its primitive root to shine and to boast. But

---

[19] The focus here is on praise not worship, and although there is so much overlap, there is not the space to discuss this at length. It is the author's view, however, that we should not assume praise is exclusively one thing and worship is another, and should not be too dogmatic in making such comparisons.

[20] The English word, worship, comes from two old English words: 'weorth', which means worth, and 'scipe' or ship, which means quality or condition. Worship, therefore, is the acknowledgment and quality of having worth.

[21] Compare: Psalm 117 (NKJV); Psalm 104: 1-2 (NKJV); Psalm 98: 4 (NKJV); Psalm 42: 5 (NKJV)

[22] Hallelujah (meaning 'praise the Lord') is an English transliteration of 'halal' (praise) and 'yah', short for Yahweh (the Lord).

in its Piel Stem (a mode of a Hebrew verb that is used to express an intensive type of action with an active voice), it means to 'praise'. In other words, in these Psalms and elsewhere, *halal* denotes a mighty explosion of enthusiasm in the act of praising. It is that deafening roar of celebration that rises up when fans witness their team scoring the winning goal in the final few moments of a game. There is no shame or concern for dignity; there is no restraint or fear of appearing foolish. In that moment, all is abandoned to the one worthy of praise. How we should boast of God's glory in similar fashion, shine out with the goodness of who He is, and erupt with excitement as we praise Him for His greatness and love! This is what *halal* means. Let everything that has breath praise the Lord in this way.

Another word that is commonly used is *yadah*. It literally means to hold your hand out in order to throw a stone or shoot an arrow, but as an intensive type of action, it means to shoot out praise, to acknowledge in public and hurl thanks to God: *'I will praise you with my whole heart; before the gods I will sing praises to you'*[23]. Here David is publically acknowledging all that God has done, praising Him with his whole heart, with extended hands. There is no mistake about his commitment to go deeper, regardless of those around him. This word is also used in 2 Chronicles 20: 19-21 (NKJV) when the Levites went out before the army praising the Lord. Again, this was an outward and public expression of exuberant praise, with hands raised up to heaven, declaring the beauty of His holiness. In every area of life including praise, what we do with our hands is important. For instance, closed hands form a fist, and this is often a sign of defence. Open hands reach out and this is often a sign of welcome and embrace. In our praising, we have the opportunity, as the Psalmist writes, to bless the Lord while we live, and lift up our (open) hands in His name, celebrating His loving kindness, which is better than life[24].

---

[23] Psalm 138: 1 (NKJV)
[24] Psalm 63: 4 (NKJV)

Then there are the musical verbs for praise. *Zamar* carries with it the idea of making music in praise to God both in the context of playing a musical instrument (Psalm 33: 2; 98: 5, NKJV), but more often singing to a musical accompaniment (Psalm 71: 22-23, NKJV). *Tehillah* is another Hebrew word meaning to sing or a song of praise, thanksgiving and adoration, and is used for example in Psalm 22: 3 (NKJV), where God manifests Himself in the midst of our praises (singing). *Pasah* means to 'break forth in song' and make a loud noise (Psalm 98: 4, NKJV); and *Shabach* means to address in a loud tone (Psalm 63: 3, NKJV).

These words are important especially as we glance through history and see how music and musical expression (through voice, sound and instrument) became the functional expression of daily life, work, and praise for the Hebrew people. Today, music has become complex and synonymous with entertainment. In the Old Testament, music was rooted in relationship with God, first in its primitive forms and then as it became a central part of temple praise. An indication of this can be found in Genesis 4, where the first musician, Jubal, is mentioned: *'He was the father of all those who play the harp and flute'*[25]. Not only is this significant in terms of his name: 'Jubal' is thought to be a derivative from the Hebrew word for 'ram', and the ram's horn (shofar) was an early instrument for the Jewish people, significant in signalling key events. But it is important also in the way he is recorded in equal measure alongside his brother Jabal, the herdsman, and Tubal-Cain, the craftsman. In other words, musicianship and musical composition was highly regarded among the earliest professions of these nomadic peoples, and continued right through the temple period into the New Testament and beyond. The point is this: from the earliest days of relationship with God, singing to the Lord and making music has always been a significant aspect of our praise.

---

[25] Genesis 4: 21 (NKJV)

We have a similar picture in the New Testament. Rooted in the Old Testament scriptures, the early church dived into the deep when it came to praising God, and the New Testament text reflects this also. After Jesus' ascension, the disciples '... *returned to Jerusalem with great joy, and were continually in the temple praising (aineo) and blessing (eulogeo) God*'[26]. *Aineo* denotes the act of expressing praise, and *eulogeo* typically refers to speech that speaks well of and gives thanks. This was a gathering of people filled with exuberant joy and great excitement, continuously giving their all to God in praise. When Paul and Silas were imprisoned in Philippi, at midnight they were praying and singing hymns to God. *Humneo* means to celebrate in song, and sing a hymn of praise. It is noteworthy that the other prisoners heard their praise[27]. When Paul enjoins the Ephesian church community to '*speak to one another in psalms and hymns and spiritual songs, singing and making melody in your heart to the Lord, giving thanks always...*'[28], the verb he uses for making melody, *psallo*, involves using a stringed instrument to accompany the singing; in other words, he was encouraging them to form a 'band'. And Paul's benediction at the end of his letter to the Romans reminds the church of the glory that is forever due to God: '*... to God alone wise, be glory through Jesus Christ forever*'[29]. This word, *doxa*, used 168 times in the New Testament, means to give glory, splendour, honour and praise.

> It is simply not possible to praise someone with the desire to bestow upon them glory, splendour and honour without the offering the whole of our being.

There are of course many more words for praise in both Old and New Testament that we could draw attention to; I have merely

---

[26] Luke 24: 52-53 (NKJV)
[27] Acts 16: 25 (NKJV)
[28] Ephesians 5: 19-20 (NKJV)
[29] Romans 16: 27 (NKJV)

highlighted a few. And whilst I recognise that this is far from being a complete study[30], the examples I have used nonetheless reflect the whole and highlight two important conclusions. Firstly, the language in both Old and New Testament demands authentic praise to be active and passionate, spoken and sung, played and sounded, outward and upward. Secondly, the language itself and the context in which the words are used strongly suggest depth and going deeper in our praise. These are not words that limit us in our praising or create walls of familiarity and restraint. We cannot fall back on such language and defend the cause of passivity. Quite the opposite: there is a boldness that breathes through these words that demands more and more by way of our commitment and action, movement and expression, passion and freedom. Our language and understanding of praise needs to reflect the 'deep in God calling to the deep in us'.

But there is another part of the answer as to why we hold back and have a proclivity for the poolside and not the sea, and I believe this lies in our misplaced perceptions: the sense that God would favour formality over freedom, restraint over release, and a contained offering more than an abandoned heart. Whether such perceptions are rooted in the fear of offending the Almighty, or the need to control what we do, the evidence of this throughout history and into the present day is quite overwhelming. I have been a chorister in a Cathedral choir, have been involved in numerous local churches (of various denominations and movements), have attended a variety of conferences and gatherings and visited churches all over the world (including China and Africa), have studied at Theological College,

---

[30] For further study, there are a number of works by the theologian, Walter Brueggermann, for example 'Israel's Praise' (Minneapolis: Fortress Press, 1988). In this book, the author begins with the premise that praise is something that is not responsive to a fixed and settled state of being, but to world-making, and this '… world-making is done by God. That is foundational to Israel's faith. But it is done through human activity which God has authorized and in which God is known to be present' (page 11).

and latterly have been ministering in the Anglican Church, and have seen first hand this spirit of restraint in each of these different experiences. It is all around us. Recently I met up with a school friend who I had not seen for some time. He came to the church where I was invited to speak, and was quite moved by the atmosphere of praise and touched by the Holy Spirit's presence. As we talked, I asked him whether he attended church, and he admitted he only went along to his local church on the 'high days and holidays'. When I asked him why, he replied that he found it too formal and 'ice-cold hearted' (his words). It is important to note that a formal setting does not imply a cold setting any more than informality suggests friendliness. However, as we spoke, it was clear to seeing a longing in him for something more.

What is it we are afraid of? What is it that we want to control and keep a lid on? God sees the heart anyway. We cannot hide from Him. If there are those who are intent on controlling our meetings, God will reveal it. If there are those who have a predisposition to disrupt, He will bring them into the light. He simply longs for us to give Him our whole heart, and trust Him in the depths of His presence. This was the issue Amos had to speak into.

> *'I hate, I despise your feast days, and I do not savour your sacred assemblies. Though you offer Me burnt offerings, I will not accept them, nor will I regard your fattened peace offerings. Take away from Me the noise of your songs, for I will not hear the melody of your stringed instruments. But let justice run down like water, and righteousness like a mighty stream*'[31].

Israel's praise had become shallow. The people favoured formality and restraint, and used this approach to cover up their disobedience

---

[31] Amos 5: 21-24 (NKJV)

and acts of injustice, and God could see though it all. Though the offerings were presented, and the feast days were celebrated, there was no depth. Jesus picks up on this too with the Pharisees and scribes, citing the prophet Isaiah: *'This people honour me with their lips, but their heart is far from Me, and in vain they worship Me teaching as doctrines the commandments of men'*[32].

The deep is calling! There is an invitation for each one of us, whatever our tradition, denomination, style or approach, to go deeper in our praise: to break free from the walls of containment that we and others have placed around ourselves; to step out into the sea with the commitment and passion of being unreserved, uncontained and even undignified; and to allow ourselves to be immersed in the waves and billows of God's love and glory as we praise Him with everything we have and all that we are.

This means praising Him with a renewed understanding; this means delighting in Him through our words, songs, and speech; this means rejoicing in Him with our musical playing, our actions and our movement, holding nothing back from the One who has given His all. It also means allowing the Holy Spirit to knit together in us this beautiful tapestry of praise, as David prays: *'Unite my heart to [revere] Your name. I will praise You, O Lord my God, with all my heart, and I will glorify Your name for evermore'*[33].

As we do this, not only will we discover more of who we are created to be in Him, and have even more reason to praise Him, but we will discover so much more of how He loves to inhabit this kind of praising, and release His power in and through us as we praise. The latter we will look at in the next chapter.

---

[32] Mark 7: 6b-7(NKJV)
[33] Psalm 86: 11-12 (NKJV)

Personal response

1. Adopting the Psalm 139: 23-24 refrain, ask God to search your heart about your approach to praise and your understanding of it, and whether you see yourself content with the 'pool' or swimming in the 'deep', or somewhere in between.
2. Ask the Holy Spirit to reveal any attitudes, fears or perceptions you have that do not come in line with His word, and to show you where you have knowingly or unknowingly judged others, held back or taken His presence for granted. Be honest with Him and with yourself. If you need to, repent, and then begin to praise Him out loud, lifting up your hands to heaven, and declaring the glory of who He is.

Decree over your life:

I command my spirit to attention and my mind and body to come in line with my spirit, and I decree: I will dive into the depths of God's presence and praise Him with all my heart, mind, soul and body, no longer restrained or restricted or content with familiarity, but passionate and free.

The Power of Praise

They went out before the army and were saying:
'Praise the Lord for His mercy endures forever'.
Now when they began to sing and to praise, the Lord set
ambushes against the people... and they were defeated.
2 Chronicles 20: 21-22 (NKJV)

THE THREAT WAS great and the danger was real. The King had been informed that a great multitude was coming against him and his people and, gripped with fear, he gathered together his people to seek the Lord in prayer and in fasting: *'O our God, will You not judge them? For we have no power against this great multitude that is coming against us; nor do we know what to do, but our eyes are fixed on you'*[1]. After he prayed, the Spirit of the Lord came upon one of those present in the midst of this assembly and he prophesied that the battle belonged to the Lord and the people should not be afraid. He also instructed them to go out and face the enemy but that they would not need to fight. In response the King and the people bowed down with faces to the ground and worshipped the Lord.

In the morning, they arose early and went to the place as instructed, and with renewed faith in God and in His deliverance, the King appointed his singers, the Levitical choir, to go before his army

---

[1] 2 Chronicles 20: 12 (NKJV)

and declare: *'Praise the Lord, for His mercy endures forever*[2]*'*. In a remarkable turn of events, as they began to sing (*rinnah*, a cry of jubilation) and to praise (*tehillah*, a song of praise and thanksgiving), the Lord set an ambush and the enemy began to fight against each other and everyone was killed. No one escaped. This vast horde made up of different tribes was defeated without Judah[3] drawing a sword; the only 'weapon' they used was their voices. When the king and the people came to take away the spoils of war, as was the common practice, they found such an abundance of valuables and precious jewels on those who had fallen, that it took them three days to collect. On the fourth day, they assembled to bless the Lord in the Valley of Berachah (meaning blessing), before returning to Jerusalem full of joy and rejoicing over their enemies. And the realm of the King was quiet, for '... *his God gave him rest all around*'[4].

This account in 2 Chronicles 20, which I have briefly summarised above, is one of my favourite stories. It is a passage that has a treasure chest of theological themes, such as faith and obedience, identity as God's people, powerlessness and retribution, prayer and fasting (to name a few), but at the heart of it presents a theology of praise, and in particular a truth and reality regarding the power of praise; namely it tells us what happens when God's people step out and praise Him in the beauty of His holiness with boldness, belief and obedience, even in the face of threat and danger. Undergirding this, it also reveals the heart of God and the power He releases towards those who abandon the familiar, break free from restraint, dive deep into His depths, and offer the kind of praise that seeks one goal: His face and His presence. But this is not unique.

In Acts Chapter 16, Paul and Silas have been thrown into the Philippian jail for exorcising a slave girl who was '... *possessed with a*

---

[2] They sang Psalm 136: 1 (NKJV)
[3] Whose name means 'praise'
[4] 2 Chronicles 20: 30 (NKJV)

spirit of divination and who brought her master much profit by fortune telling'[5]. Having been flogged and placed in the inner cell with feet fastened in the stocks, at midnight they are praying and singing hymns to God, with the other prisoners listening to them, when suddenly there was a great earthquake. The foundations of the prison were shaken, the doors opened, everyone's chains were loosened, and the outcome was that the jailer's life was saved (physically and spiritually) and Paul and Silas were set free. Their praise evoked God to act and save them.

Augustine, one of the great early church fathers, takes this theme up in Book 1 of his 'Confessions'. He writes that despite sin and suffering, the instinct in humankind is to praise God '… for the thought of you stirs him so deeply that he cannot be content unless he praises you because you made us for yourself, and our hearts find no peace unless they rest in you'. It is little known that this statement, which we often hear cited (especially the latter part), is actually based on his personal experience of the power of praise. On one occasion, when the congregation at Augustine's local church in Hippo were praising God, a young man was healed of a disease. The next day the young man's sister was also healed and '… they shouted God's praises without words, but with such noise that our ears could scarcely bear it'[6]. There was great rejoicing.

In the Middle Ages, we have no shortage of examples of God releasing power in the midst of praise. One notable writer is Richard Rolle, whose own experience is testimony to God's active involvement. He writes: '… I want to give [God] unceasing praise. In tribulations, in troubles, in persecutions, He has given me comfort; … so Jesus, I want to be praising you always, such is my joy. When I was down

---

[5] Acts 16: 16 (NKJV)
[6] P Hinnerbusch cited this example in his book, 'Praise a way of life', Ann Arbor: word of life, 1976, p47-48.

and out you stooped to me ...'.[7] Many more examples could be cited concerning the 'reformation with Luther, the Quakers with George Fox, Methodism with Wesley, the Plymouth Brethren with Darby and Graves, the Salvation Army with William Booth ...'.[8] to name but a few.

The 20th century to the present day certainly has its lion share of these praise and power encounters, especially in terms of empirical data and recording these experiences. In 1906, a 'Pentecostal explosion' erupted in Azusa Street, Los Angeles, where people were saved and immersed in the Holy Spirit, released into jubilant and spontaneous praise, healed and set free, and sent out into the mission field. William Seymour, pastor of the church, wrote in the 'Apostolic Faith' magazine in September of that year: 'The people had nothing to do but wait on the Lord and praise Him, and they commenced speaking in tongues, as they did at Pentecost, and the Spirit sang songs through them ... It is spreading everywhere'; and he ended, '... we are going on to get more of the power of God'[9].

This sense of heart-felt praise, especially in song, was an important feature of the Charismatic movement which began in the early nineteen-sixties, and largely fell within the historic denominations – a key difference from the Pentecostal movement – and later the Protestant Evangelical Renewal which emerged in the early nineteen-eighties with John Wimber as a key figure and is still prevalent today. An example that David Fellingham cites in his article 'Praise and the Kingdom', expresses well the two movements' expected outcome of praise that releases the presence and power of God: 'A group of young people from a church in Basingstoke were returning from

---

[7] Richard Rolle (translated C Wolters), 'the fire of love', Londond: Penguin Books, 1988, p.94
[8] Cited in L McClung, 'Azuza street and beyond', South Plainfield: Bridge Publishing Inc. 1986, p.4
[9] Cited in L McClung, 1986, p.24

London when a car forced their minibus in a lay-by. He writes: "A menacing gang tried to break in, one of them standing on the running board and declaring evil intentions ... The young people in the minibus began to worship, singing and praising in tongues. The effect was not immediate, but gradually the gang left... An ugly and potentially vicious situation had been diffused by the power of God... Through the praises of the young people, God's presence was released into the situation"[10].

Then there is my own experience of the power of praise. In 1997, I was still teaching at a senior school in London. On one occasion in September that year, I was cycling to work and as I often did, was singing songs of praise out loud[11] when I heard a terrible crash behind me. I was half way up Trapps Lane, New Malden, when I looked over my shoulder to see glass hurtling towards me. Without having time to think, I swerved off the road and was able to take cover behind a wall[12]. I heard a further crash and the screeching sound of metal on the tarmac. As I got off my bike and went to see what had happened, I saw a car overturned in the middle of the road, the front part flattened and billows of smoke coming from the engine. My immediate thought concerned the wellbeing of the driver. As I approached the car wondering whether he or she was alive or not, and whether the car would catch fire, I saw the driver move. In fact, she was crawling into the back, and as I pulled the door open, I helped her out and lead her away to safety.

---

[10] Taken from D. Fellingham, 'Worship restored', Eastbourne, Kingsway, 1987

[11] Only this time, I was unashamedly singing particularly loudly as I had just attended a Vineyard Conference, learnt some amazing new songs, and had experienced God's presence in a powerful and transforming way.

[12] At the exact point of turning, the high pavement had stopped, and in the goodness of God, there was a private drive that enabled me to get out of danger and a brick wall that protected me from the flying debris of glass.

Amazingly, apart from the shock of what had just happened, the woman was not hurt, cut or bruised in any way. This in itself was remarkable, but even more so when we heard the series of events from the lady who was driving behind her up the lane. According to this eyewitness, the driver had been swerving about at the foot of the hill – clearly she had passed out momentarily – and then had unconsciously accelerated up the hill heading straight for me. A few feet away from hitting me at speed, the left wing of her car crashed into a street lamp causing not only the top part of the lamp to fall, strewing glass everywhere, but her car to overturn and skid into the middle of the road on its roof. We were both very fortunate to be alive. Yet as we waited for the police to arrive I sensed an incredible peace of God in my whole being and covering that place, and knew beyond any doubt that our protection was linked inextricably to the praises I had previously been singing. I had been praising God and praying for protection and He had graciously intervened in a powerful way. Not surprisingly, after being released by the police (who were astounded there were no dead bodies to deal with, especially after hearing the witness' first hand account), I continued my journey full of praise and rejoicing. I certainly had reason to praise, and found myself singing a new song with even more abandonment, freedom and joy.

There is very good reason for citing all these examples from the Bible and from church history, including personal testimony, and it is simply this: when we praise God as He has created us to do, there is power. When we make room for God to be present in our midst and delight in Him with our whole being, He releases a power that defeats our enemies, opens doors to prisons, heals and comforts, saves and protects.

This is the power of praise.

It is not our power to control, manipulate, or to use to our own advantage; some try to do that and the consequences are disastrous for all concerned. This power is always and only God's to administer.

He is the source and He has to be present. But when He comes and moves in power in the midst of our praising, something wonderful and beautiful is found, which draws us deeper and longing for more:

> *'Have you not known? Have you not heard? The everlasting God, the Lord, the Creator of the ends of the earth, neither faints nor is weary. His understanding is unsearchable. He gives power to the weak, and to those who have no might He increases strength. Even the youths shall faint and be weary, And the young men shall utterly fall, But those who wait on the* L*ord* *shall renew their strength; they shall mount up with wings like eagles, they shall run and not be weary, they shall walk and not faint'*[13].

Why is this? Simply in the glory of who He is, the Lord can no more be contained or reserved than a tidal wave can be captured in a small bottle. It is not in His nature to be restrained or restricted. There is nothing familiar about His will and His ways. As the prophet Isaiah declares throughout this whole chapter, His understanding is unsearchable, His power is incomparable, and His love towards us has no measure. So when we wait on Him nothing less than 'power' - the dynamic of His love and presence - can be expected and experienced.

The question for us is: why then do we not see and experience more of His power when we praise?

There are of course multiple complexities to answering such a question, not least in understanding our specific context and surroundings. But there are common indicators that help us not only to have a greater understanding, but also enable us to create an

---

[13] Isaiah 40:28-31 (NKJV)

economy of space to experience more, by the grace of God; and the starting line is the gateway of praise.

In Psalm 100 verse 4, we read: *'Enter into His gates with thanksgiving, and into His courts with praise'* (NKJV). The context of 'entering' is making a joyful shout to the Lord, vocally and outwardly, serving with gladness and coming before His presence with singing, knowing who it is we are praising[14]. Every verb used here expects action, energy and intensity. This is not a casual gathering around the piano, singing some of our favourite songs; this verse invokes commitment and passion. How often do we arrive at a meeting or service, distracted by earlier events, and open our mouths to sing when our minds are elsewhere. But neither is it an excuse for extremist behaviour, as if the only way to get God's attention is to sing louder, move about more vigorously, and metaphorically 'beat' ourselves until His presence falls[15]. God is not looking for lukewarm, but neither is He after burnt out. In fact, He loves it when we approach Him like children:

> *'Out of the mouths of babes and nursing infants,*
> *You have perfected praise'*[16].

Citing Psalm 8 verse 2, Jesus gives us a life-changing, all encompassing and transforming insight into what our approach to praise should look like. In this passage, not only is He challenging the attitude of indignation towards others; in this situation, the indignation of the chief priests and scribes towards what the children are saying: *'Hosanna to the Son of David'* (NKJV). But He is revealing the delight of His heavenly Father towards us when we praise Him like these little children.

---

[14] Psalm 100: 1-3 (NKJV)
[15] Compare 1 Kings 18: 27 – 39 (NKJV)
[16] Matthew 21: 16 (NKJV)

Such praise is 'perfected praise'.

The word for 'perfected', *katartizo*, means to repair, restore, and join together completely; to make perfect. What a message of hope and renewal for the church today! Whatever the condition we are currently facing, whether formal or informal, contained or free, there is always the possibility of moving closer towards 'perfected praise'. However, the only way we can repair and restore our offering of praise, and to enter into God's presence where His power is known and experienced, is to come before Him as children.

It is important though that we do not confuse the notion of being children with the idea of being immature, or mistake the nature of child-like with childish behaviour. Our two girls are now grown up, but we have so many wonderful recorded memories of when they were little children, especially when we made the space for them simply to be themselves. Both of them were so expressive and excitable, so adventurous and loud, so free and creative. Everything in their world-view expanded and grew, and the possibilities in their eyes were limitless. It was wonderful to see, and still is! But then they were completely dependant upon us as parents, for food, clothing, warmth, safety, provision, protection and love. Dependency is not a weakness. Our children learnt their language from us, and imitated the words we spoke. They grew to understand boundaries and came to value the things that were important to us. As they developed their own personalities, they loved as we modelled love, responded to the things we responded to, and shared in every area of the life we lived. This is simply being a child.

'Out of the mouths' always reflects what is in the heart[17].

---

[17] Consider Jesus' teaching in Mark 7: 1-17 (NKJV)

Jesus is opening up a reality for each one of us, whatever our age, to attain that same kind of dependency on our Heavenly Father as His children: to learn His language and speak His words; to know His will and value His ways; and as we grow in maturity, to love as He loves us. Jesus also exemplified this perfectly, and showed us how it can be done. Always the Son, he says to us: *'Most assuredly, I say to you, the Son can do nothing of Himself, but what He sees the Father do; for whatever He does, the Son does in like manner. For the Father loves the Son and shows Him all things that He Himself does'*[18]. Paul too, picks up this theme when he writes to the church in Philippi: *'Finally, brethren, whatever things are true, whatever things are noble, whatever things are just, whatever things are pure, whatever things are lovely, whatever things are of good report, if there is any virtue and if anything is praiseworthy – meditate on these things. The things which you learned and received and heard and saw in me, these do and the God of peace will be with you'*[19].

This is how we need to come before our Heavenly Father; as His children. A paraphrase of Psalm 8 verse 2 could then be: *'As children make a joyful shout to the Lord; as little ones serve Him with gladness; as infants come before His presence with singing'*, and then enter His gates with thanksgiving and His courts with praise. There is no other way! No alternative route! God has made it so, and 'praise' with 'thanksgiving' is the gateway to knowing His power.

In the Bible times, gates have great significance. Besides protecting a community and keeping the enemy out, they were places where business transactions took place, courts convened, and proclamations were made. If you controlled the gates of your enemy, you took control over the city[20]. It was not hard then for the Hebrew people to understand the significance of the prophetic word, given to Isaiah,

---

[18] John 5: 19-20 (NKJV)
[19] Philippians 4: 8-9 (NKJV)
[20] Compare Genesis 22: 17, where part of the blessing given to Abraham was for him and his descendants to '… possess the gate of their enemies' (NKJV).

announcing the restoration of Jerusalem and its gates: *'the City of our Lord, Zion of the Holy One of Israel … But you shall call your walls Salvation and your gates Praise'*[21]. With hindsight, we can see this pointing ahead to Jesus, the perfect embodiment of this vision and the New Jerusalem coming out of heaven[22]. But as a prophetic word, the message is clear and simple for even children to grasp: God has surrounded Himself by a wall called 'salvation' and has made access to Himself through a gateway, and the name of the gate is called 'praise'.

So many times people come before God bringing their requests and concerns, complaints and problems, hoping for His power to move. You may identify with this approach yourself. But this is not the gateway into knowing His power. Too many times we stand before God corporately crying out to Him with petitions and supplications, longing for His intervention and action. We may relate to this week-by-week in our services. But this is not the gateway into releasing His power. As revealed in His word, and declared by the Son Himself, it is only as we come to Him with a child-like leap of joy and a song of delight, simply by being with our Heavenly Dad, true to who we are (with no pretence or false motive), that we find ourselves immersed in the deep of His presence and experience the depths of His power. This is praise how God has designed it to be. And when we enter the gates of praise for the right reason and in a right relationship, we can be sure that sooner or later, His power will manifest itself in a myriad of ways.

> His power comes and sets people free when we praise.

I have already given examples above of amazing things that have happened when we make room for praise. One of the things I have noticed more and more, as we have gone deeper and journeyed towards this 'perfected praise', is the way the Holy Spirit heals people

---

[21] Isaiah 60: 14 and 18 (NKJV)
[22] John's vision in Revelation 21 (NKJV).

during times of praise. Without a word of prayer being spoken, we have witnessed people being healed of viruses, migraines and allergies. We have seen depression lift off and broken hearts restored. As the atmosphere of praise continues after the service and as refreshments are being served, we have seen people continue to receive healing. One recent testimony, in May 2016, was when a visitor came to our morning service. He had been deaf in one of his ears for four years. As the church was singing and exalting the Lord, suddenly he starts laughing and crying out loud. He was a big man so his outburst could hardly go unnoticed. With great delight and celebration, he announced to those around him that his ears had opened up spontaneously as we were praising. Later on his testimony was shared before the congregation, so that together we could give God the glory. The power of praise!

> His power comes and the enemy has to flee when we praise.

Praise is also a powerful spiritual weapon against the schemes and attacks of the devil and his demons. It releases power from heaven that silences his lies and releases the captive and the oppressed. The powers of darkness are powerless when it comes to our child-like praise, and Psalm 8 verse 2 and Matthew 21 verse 16 give us the mandate for this: *'Out of the mouth of babes and nursing infants You have ordained strength, because of Your enemies, that You may silence the enemy and the avenger'* (NKJV). The Psalmist, David, recognises that we are not dealing with a single enemy, but against 'enemies' plural. The same forces of darkness that Paul writes about in Ephesian 6: *'For we do not wrestle against flesh and blood, but against principalities, against powers, against the rulers of this dark age, against spiritual hosts of wickedness in the heavenly places'*[23]; and David (like Paul) certainly had his fair share of this kind of attack. Yet he knows that there is a way through; and

---

[23] Ephesians 6: 12 (NKJV)

that is with child-like strength that is ordained by God. However, it is many years later that Jesus gives further depth into this revelation, and in doing so discloses how this ordained strength comes into effect when we move into the realm of praise; perfected praise. In other words, praise is the ordained power to still those principalities that come against us. But such praise has to come from the heart of child-like faith; a mystery Jesus Himself rejoices in: *'I thank you, Father, Lord of heaven and earth, that You have hidden these things from the wise and prudent and revealed them to babes. Even so, Father, for so it seemed good in your sight'*[24].

A few years ago, our church went through a very difficult and painful time, and certainly the forces of darkness were at work. Knowing the church was suffering, I contacted a friend who had a long established ministry in deliverance, and asked her to join me, with a few selected church members, as we sought the Lord. We began the evening with praise, and committed ourselves to giving time to singing and thanksgiving, and during that time, my friend sensed very strongly that we were dealing with two demonic strongholds that had gripped the church for many years: pride and idolatry. As we stood together, repented on behalf of the church and then commanded these strongholds to leave, we heard two audible and loud, distinct and sudden, cracks in the roof. My initial thoughts were that the roof was falling in so forceful was the sound; and we had only repaired it recently. Checking the ceiling that night, and on closer inspection the next day, there was no damage to either the outside or inside of the church. However, when the congregation gathered together the next Sunday for our morning service, the atmosphere was completely different. There was a noticeable lightness and peace, a humility and grace towards one another, and a number of people came up to me afterwards and asked: what has happened to our church? This lightness continues to this day. The power of praise!

---

[24] Luke 10:21 (NKJV)

His power comes and we hear God speak when we praise.

Recently, we had a meeting for leaders in our church. As is the practice for such gatherings, we are learning to give more time to praise (as opposed to the diving straight into the business of the meeting, important though it is). As we were praising, speaking out and singing, one of our leaders had a vision, like an old movie picture. This is what she wrote down for me: she saw a vision of a giant keyboard (like something that you would find in Lilliput/Gulliver's Travels) and each member of the Church family was allocated a key. As she watched, individuals began to jump up and down on their allocated key with great joy and excitement. And as everyone began to jump – each on their own key - the most incredible music began to emanate from the keyboard which ministered to the Father's heart and to the community all around.

She then sensed this moving picture was for us as a Church family: that each member has a key (or a note) to play in the incredible symphony that the Father has written and that there is a call for each person to find their voice and collaborate, with joy, to bring about the plans and purposes that the Father has for us as a Church family at such a time as this.

As you can imagine, this was an incredibly encouraging and uplifting word to receive by faith, and already we are seeing the fruit of it. But this is not an isolated event. There is a growing expectation that when we praise, the Holy Spirit releases revelation for us, or for others. When we lift up our hearts, voices and hands in adoration, He releases His *rhema*[25] word; and just as Jesus told us when He was responding to the temptations of the devil, it brings life to our

---

[25] *Rhema* is a word that is spoken. It is the word used in Matthew 4: 4 (NKJV)

living. We come alive in His power as we hear His voice: *'Man shall not live by bread alone, but by every word that proceeds from the mouth of God'*[26]. This is the power of praise.

> His power comes and we are clothed with His presence when we praise.

In Matthew Chapter 5, Jesus makes a number of extraordinary statements; one of them comes in verses 14-16. Speaking about light, he tells those who were listening to him: *'You are the light of the world'*[27]. He then instructs these believers not to put their light under a basket, and finishes by saying: *'Let your light shine before men, that they may see your good works and glorify your father in heaven'*[28]. We have seen already that one of the most common Hebrew words for praise, *halal*, which would also have been frequently spoken or sung in the synagogues and temple during Jesus' time, means to boast or to shine. In the context of the Beatitudes and concluding with the exhortation to 'rejoice and be exceedingly glad', Jesus then continues with the theme to 'shine'. The link is not co-incidental. Clearly Jesus is concerned with what we do, and how this witnesses to those around us. Good and beautiful works give glory to the Father, and few would overlook such an interpretation of this passage. However, in making this statement, Jesus is also revealing something about what we carry; namely when we 'rejoice' and are 'exceedingly glad'[29], we are clothed with a shining presence and power that the world needs to see and encounter.

---

[26] Matthew 4: 4 (NKJV)
[27] Matthew 5: 14 (NKJV)
[28] Matthew 5: 16 (NKJV)
[29] Both these words, *chairo* (rejoice) and *agallieo* (exceedingly glad) denote the outward expression and jubilance of that which is praise worship and joyful.

Lighting a candle and setting it on a lampstand not only gives light to the room but also emanates warmth. From a distance, one only knows the benefit of the light. However close up one sees the strength of the light as well as feels the heat around the candle; it is only by being close to the flame that you are clothed in the warmth. Praise is such a garment. In fact, the prophet Isaiah speaks of it as being '... *a garment of praise for the spirit of heaviness*' (NKJV).

Over the years I have come to know many people, including my beautiful wife, who I would consider people of praise: committed and passionate, longing to go deeper into the depths of God's love, and willing to be child-like in their approach as they enter the gates of praise. Without exception, not only are they inspiring, but incredibly warm to be around. Praise has the power to lift of heaviness and burn away what we might call today the spirit of depression. Clearly the heart of our Saviour then, as now, is to be so clothed in His power, that wherever we go and whatever we do, our '*halal*' life of praise shines for His glory, and this garment of warmth and fire reaches those who we are close to. This too is the power of praise.

> His power comes and we are one with Him and with each other when we praise.

Unity is a word that we often use in Christian circles to express oneness and togetherness. This is of course so important, especially at a time when there seems to be so much division and separation in the church both in terms of theology and praxis. However, as much as unity may be sought and worked at between different groups and factions, the Bible is clear as to its source and nature. Its source is the Holy Spirit and its nature is what Paul calls the bond of peace: '... *keep the unity of the Spirit in the bond of peace*'[30]. In other words, when the focus is on striving towards human agreement and even

---

[30] Ephesians 4: 3 (NKJV); unity, *henotes*, means oneness.

compromise, unity can never be fully realised. It is only when the Holy Spirit is present in the meeting, and His peace is covering the gathering, that this spiritual oneness can be known and experienced. And when this happens in the midst of praise, as we gather as one, His power is gloriously released.

Joshua Chapter 6 is a notable example. It was on the seventh day when the priests blew their trumpets and the people shouted with a 'great shout[31]' of praise in oneness and togetherness, in obedience to God's word, that the walls of the city of Jericho came crashing down, and the city was completely destroyed. Another example, in a different context, is 2 Chronicles 5, when all the trumpeters and singers came together '... *as one, to make one sound to be heard in praising and thanking the Lord*'[32]. The presence of the Lord fell so weightily that no one could stand to minister as the glory cloud of the Lord filled the house. Amazing power!

I have not yet had such an encounter[33], but there have been many times when the Holy Spirit's presence has brought our meeting to our knees. On one occasion recently we were so caught up in the holiness of God, that we physically felt a strong wind blow through a closed door and hover a foot above the ground. One by one we fell to our knees or bowed face down to the ground, and experienced the most extraordinary and beautiful weighty presence of love and grace. But what was significant was that no one in the room missed out; there was an oneness in our response and a unity in the Spirit. Afterwards we could hardly speak but we all knew we had experienced something very powerful. The psalmist is right: '*Behold, how good and how pleasant it is for brethren to dwell together in unity*'[34]!

---

[31] Joshua 6:20 (NKJV); 'shout', *truwah*, means to shout loudly with rejoicing.
[32] 2 Chronicles 5:13 (NKJV)
[33] I believe this should be the goal of all our praise and worship
[34] Psalm 133 (NKJV)

> His power comes and we know we are loved when
> we praise.

This is both the solid rock and the mountain peak of praise; knowing the power of the Father's love as we lift our hearts and voices to Him. Paul strips 'love' right down in 1 Corinthians Chapter 13 when he speaks of gifts without love or deeds without love or even sacrifice without love amounting to nothing and profiting no one; and concludes with the well known verse: *'And now abide faith, hope, love these three; but the greatest of these is love'*[35]. Of course, love is the greatest gift. But there is a depth to this gift of love that is often missing in our praising, and in those who gather to praise: namely, love is not only a gift of salvation which we receive by faith[36], or a choice we make to follow, and in response sing songs about such love. Of course we do, and this is right. But there is so much more. This love is the deep and intimate knowledge of the Father's love for us, and our love for Him, through the saving love of Jesus and the empowering love of the Holy Spirit.

On Sunday 11th December 2016, I was at the front of church singing and shouting out my praises, with hands reached out, enjoying the freedom as the church was lead deeper into God's presence, when suddenly I felt someone take hold of my hand. For a moment my eyes remained closed, imagining it was my wife or someone close by praying for me. But after a while, I looked around me and no one was praying[37]. I continued in praise and my hand was still being held. In fact the grip was getting tighter and, even more unusually, the way I was held felt like a 'giant' reaching down and taking hold of me, as a father would reach down and take hold of the hand of a toddler when crossing the road. In that moment, I knew it was

---

[35] 1 Corinthians 13: 13 (NKJV)
[36] John 3: 16 (NKJV)
[37] It was later confirmed by those behind me that no one took hold of my hand or prayed for me during this time.

my Heavenly Father, and subsequently enjoyed the most incredible encounter as He began speaking and pouring out His love.

As the singing quietened down and the band continued to play gently, I was lead by the Holy Spirit to minister into this experience, having briefly explained what had happened to me, and simply said over and over again: 'Put your hand in the hand of the One who loves you', as the Holy Spirit came to rest on each person. At some point, I also said: 'I believe this means something specific to someone here'.

Four weeks later, after the service, I was introduced to a young man by his father. His father is a regular and committed member of our church, but for many years, his son had completely wandered off from the Lord. This young man had been very ill and was going through a difficult time in his life, and during the week (prior to Sunday 11th December) he was lying on his bed when he finally cried out to God for help. What happened was so moving; he had tears in his eyes as he shared. He told me that someone took hold of his hand, and he knew it was God, and in that moment gave his life to Jesus. Sunday 11th December was the first Sunday service he had come to church since being a child, and was amazed when I shared the testimony of the Father holding my hand; he knew this was the confirmation he needed as he allowed the Father to pour His love into his life. How amazing it is to know that we can discover the depth of God's love for us, as His children, in the midst of our praise. This is the power of praise.

When the great composer Handel was composing his masterpiece, the Messiah, he barricaded himself in his room. When he came to the climax of the composition, which is the Hallelujah chorus, he told a friend afterwards what his experience was like in that room. His words were: "It seemed as if heaven came down and filled my soul". That certainly deserves a 'Hallelujah'!

When we know the One we have been created to praise and the realm He loves to dwell in; when we know the reason for praise and the unfathomable depths we can enjoy; when we know the gateway and come to Him as His children, we will discover the incredible power of praise. It will amaze us, delight us, overwhelm us, confound us, and change us for His glory and the honour of His name. This is a mystery God reveals only to His children.

Do not praise God because of the miracles, signs and wonders, but know when you do praise Him with all your heart, these things will come.

Do not praise Him because you are in the heat of the battle, but know when you do praise Him for the beauty of His Holiness, victory after victory will be won.

Do not praise Him because you will get a prophetic word and hear His voice, but know when you do praise His glorious name, He will speak.

Do not praise Him because others will see His power rest on you, but know when you do praise Him with your gaze fixed on His face, He will shine through you.

Do not praise Him because you want to experience His presence, but know when you do praise Him in unity and oneness, His glory will fall in power.

Do not praise Him because of what you get from Him as His child, but know when you do praise Him delighting in your Heavenly Father, He will bestow blessing upon blessing.

And keep praising, even in the midst of pain and difficulty, and especially in those times of suffering. This is the sacrifice of praise, which we will discuss in the next chapter.

Personal response

1. Read Psalm 100 and take some time reflecting on the verbs in the Psalm, and the way they imply action, energy and intensity. Ask the Holy Spirit to show you how you approach praising Him, both in the secret place and in public. Be honest with Him and with yourself.
2. '*Out of the mouths of babes and nursing infants, you have perfected praise*' (Matthew 21:16, NKJV). What needs repairing or restoring in your offering of praise, so that you can move closer to perfected praise? Be intentional about praising God out loud, whether you are on your way to work, in your home, on your bike or as you are walking.

Decree over your life:

I command my spirit to attention and my mind and body to come in line with my spirit, and I decree: I will enter through the gateway of praise into God's presence where His power is known and experienced, with a child-like leap of joy and with songs of thanksgiving, knowing the Lord is good, His mercy is everlasting, and His truth endures to all generations.

The Sacrifice of Praise

Therefore by [Jesus] let us continually offer the sacrifice of praise to God, that is, the fruit of our lips, giving thanks to His name.
Hebrews 13: 15 (NKJV)

SOME WORDS IN scripture have a habit of making life difficult for us[1]. Have you noticed? Or to be more specific, the inclusion of certain words in particular contexts and verses can make our lives really testing! It would be so much easier if they were not included or could be re-interpreted in a different way. Take the word 'love' for example. It is a wonderful and powerful word, and we find it in so many beautiful passages in both Old and New Testaments. In Koine Greek, the language our New Testament was primarily written in, it has four different meanings[2]. Then there are the eternal truths to do with love, such as 1 John 4: 16: *'God is love and He who abides in love abides in God, and God in him'* (NKJV). But place this word 'love' in the context of Matthew 5: 43-44, and then we have a real challenge on our hands: *'You have heard it said, you shall love your neighbour and hate your enemy, but I* [Jesus speaking] *say to you, love your enemies'* (NKJV). And in case we may be struggling to understand what He is saying, Jesus reinforces this command by

---

[1] This is not a criticism, just an observation, based on experience.
[2] *Philia*, is a friendship love; *eros* is a physical/sexual love; *storge* is a preference love; and *agape* is a self-sacrificing love.

adding *'... and bless those who curse you, do good to those who hate you, and pray for those who spitefully use you and persecute you, that you may be sons of your Father in heaven'* (NKJV). Now that is a word that challenges our attitudes and tests the way we relate to others! It would of course be so much easier in the context of enemies if it were not there, or supplemented with a few additional words, such as: 'love your enemies only on Sundays', or 'love your enemies if your name is Peter'.

Laying aside any sense of hardship or my poor humour, we know of course why 'love' and other similar kinds of words, such as forgiveness, are included in the contexts they are written; as Paul says to Timothy: *'All scripture is given by inspiration of God, and is profitable for doctrine, for reproof, for correction, and for instruction in righteousness, that the man of God may be complete, thoroughly equipped for every good work'*[3]. All scripture is 'God-breathed'[4] and is profitable. In other words, God knows what is best for us and His world, and has revealed this to us through His Word and by His Spirit[5], so that we can attain the best, and *'press toward the goal for the prize of the upward call of God in Christ Jesus'*[6]. Loving our enemies is better than hating them; forgiving others is better for us than living a life of unforgiveness.

There is another word that is equally as testing which appears at the end of the Epistle to the Hebrews. In the concluding remarks to his readers, the author imparts an important revelation about praise, and in the process, like the 'love example' above, includes a word we cannot ignore or re-interpret. The word is 'continually': *'Therefore by [Jesus] let us continually offer the sacrifice of praise to*

---

[3] 2 Timothy 3: 16-17 (NKJV)
[4] Other Bible versions such as the New International Version, translate *theopneustos* as 'God-breathed'.
[5] Refer to John 4: 21-24 (NKJV)
[6] Philippians 3:14 (NKJV)

God, that is, the fruit of our lips, giving thanks to His name[7]. On the surface it seems quite harmless enough, but when given due care and attention, it presents an unshakable requirement and challenge; namely to continually offer to God the sacrifice of praise. The latter phrase will be addressed later on in this chapter. But in terms of the breadth and extent, this word 'continually', *diapantos*, has enormous significance for each one of us.

Our English rendition of the word would innately include the notion of 'always' and 'all the time'. It would also have the sense of that which 'does not cease'; although within this 'ceaseless time-scale' there may be intervals such as one drop of rain following another in quick succession. But in the textual setting here, it literally means 'through it all'[8].

> Therefore, by Jesus, let us through it all offer our sacrifice of praise to God, that is, the fruit of our lips, giving thanks to His name.

Let me ask then the inevitable question: what happens to our praise when we encounter distraction, temptation, difficulty, suffering, loss, and even come face to face with persecution? Or to put it another way, when the storms come against us, who is the first to lose out on our praise?

Admittedly there is an assumption behind these two questions; namely the 'cause and effect' cycle that often manifests itself in our offering of praise. When the storm comes, the effect is often we neglect to offer to God praise that is rightfully due to Him. Or when we encounter distraction, temptation, difficulty, suffering, loss, and even come face to face with persecution, the outcome is often we cease to praise God. If anything, we blame Him. And there

---

[7] Hebrews 13:15 (NKJV)
[8] *Dia* is through, and *pantos* means all.

is good reason in scripture for making such an assumption, as Jesus reveals in his teachings. For example, in the Parable of the Sower, we see how the work of the devil, the tribulation and persecution, and the cares of the world cause us to withdraw from God, and have His word 'choked' out of us.[9] Without reading too much into this parable, it is not unreasonable to assume that what is also missing and 'choked out' is praise. How many people do we know, who have turned away from God, or even denied faith in Jesus, continue to praise Him? In my experience - and I know many people like that - the answer is 'none'! His praise simply does not feature in their daily thoughts, language, actions or decisions. God is often the first to lose out on our praise. This may be something you relate to yourself!

But there is another aspect to this assumption of a 'cause and effect' cycle, and the Parable of the Lost Son in Luke Chapter 15 helps draw this out. Jesus begins by telling us that a certain man had two sons[10]. Attention is often given to the younger son whose 'prodigal' living kept him far from communion with His Father; how glorious his return. But in the context of praise, the elder son highlights a dynamic at work; namely, though he stayed in communion with His Father, the effect of his younger brother's return caused him to refuse to join in and celebrate. In other words, he was angry and did not feel like rejoicing with his Father's household and the angels in heaven that *'this son who was lost is now found'*[11]. In his mind, he had good reason not to 'party'. How often do we hold onto such reasons, whether they are sourced in our anger, hurt, disappointment or pain?

But in citing the elder son's response, Jesus is revealing a behavioural pattern that was prevalent in the religious setting then as it is today; the right which we believe belongs to us, and to us alone, to choose and control when and how we praise. Sociologists might call this

---

[9] Read Mark 4: 1-20 (NKJV)
[10] Luke 15: 11 (NKJV)
[11] Luke 15: 10-32 (NKJV)

'right' independence; psychologists might name it individualism; philosophers might refer to it as free will. However, I believe the Bible calls it sin, *hamartano*, which literally means to 'miss the mark'[12]. In other words, if we imagine that the God of the Universe is worthy of praise only when we are in the mood, or if life is going well for us, we are missing the mark. If we live as if the King of Kings is deserving of our offering when we have the space and time in our diaries for Him and we dictate the format, we are missing the mark. Of course, God has given us free will and it is not in His nature to force our hand, especially when it comes to praising Him; in that sense it is our 'right'. But how far have we come from the truth if our practice lines up with such a belief? How much are we missing the centre of God's will for our lives if we limit the extent and quality of our praise, depending on circumstances, commitments and feelings? Sadly I have known people who have fallen into this category.

Added to all of the above, there are many times in our lives when tragedy falls upon us outside of our own choices, emotions and control. From time to time we all face the suffering of illness and the grief of loved ones passing away; we all share in life's difficulties and are victims of other people's bad behaviour, to a greater and lesser degree. The challenges and attacks often come upon us like a thief in the night without warning. Even in church settings the pain that comes from division, dishonouring, and disruption can be so great. It is both natural and understandable that in these moments we cry out to God - as we see the Psalmists do many times - and say to Him: where are you when I need you? Why have you not prevented this from happening to me? Why are you so far from helping me[13]?

However, the problem comes not when we cry out to God per se but when the cause that initiates the 'cry of the heart' moves us into the 'silence of the cry', and the effect is we cease from asking

---

[12] For example, see Romans *3: 23* (NKJV)
[13] Psalm 22: 1 (NKJV). Also read Psalm 71, and the Book of Habakkuk.

and seeking, and end up distancing ourselves from God altogether. This was partly what the writer to the Hebrews was concerned about when he encouraged his readers to continually praise. In that situation, there were some Jewish believers who were considering walking away from their newfound faith in Jesus, in order to avoid persecution.

Some time ago, my wife and I were going through a very difficult time in our lives, and some close friends of ours invited us to attend a church service they were going to; when I say 'invite', it was more like 'drag along' (for which we were and are enormously grateful). We were both in such emotional torment. At the end of the service, they lead us to the front to be prayed for, and a lady started by saying to Heather: 'I sense the Father saying I never said it would be easy but I did say I will always be with you'. Even now I can feel the emotion of that moment as the Holy Spirit ministered into our hearts and we discovered afresh the depths of His love and His continual promise: *'You will do everything you have promised; Lord, your love is eternal. Complete the work that you have begun'*[14].

Suffering is never easy to face whatever its nature. Life is constantly throwing up one challenge after another and we should never minimalise its effect on us or other people. Jesus knew suffering all too well as He willingly walked the path that lead to the cross, bearing the sins of all humanity upon Himself as He was crucified for our sin, so that by His death we might die to sin and rise with Him[15]. He was not understating the reality when he said: *'... narrow is the gate and difficult is the way, which leads to life, and there are few*

---

[14] Psalm 138: 8 (Good News Translation). This verse was given to us at our wedding, and God has encouraged us with it at key points in our lives together.

[15] Read the prophetic word in Isaiah 53: 3-9 (NKJV) and 1 Peter: 2: 21-25 (NKJV)

who find it'[16]. It is difficult. But by God's grace and in His strength, there is a way through to recalibrate the cause and effect cycle, so that when difficulty comes, the effect in us is to keep praising. There is a means by which the storms we encounter come and go, but through it all, the fruit of our lips continually praise God with thanksgiving.

This way is called the sacrifice of praise.

The word for 'sacrifice' in the Greek text here is *thusia*, and it means to kill and slaughter for the purpose of an offering. In other words, something has to 'die' as we bring our offering.

From the earliest chapters in the Bible, we see 'sacrifices' being offered to God. The first recorded sacrifice is found in Genesis Chapter 4, when Cain brings the fruit of his hands to the Lord, and Abel offers the fruit of his heart, the sacrifice of the first born of his flock. We are told that the Lord looked with favour on Abel's offering, but did not accept Cain's and the result was Cain murdering his brother out of jealousy. Why? Because his offering involved no cost to life! Religious division invariably occurs because those who come to God with pride and human endeavour are aggressive to those who seek God with humility and truth. Sadly, this spirit of Cain is still around in the world and church today.

By contrast to Cain's offering we read of another sacrifice in Genesis Chapter 22. Abraham is asked by God to go to the land of Moriah and offer his son, Isaac, as a burnt offering to the Lord. Having travelled a great distance and waited many years before having a son - he was one hundred years old[17] - Isaac is born. Isaac, whose name means 'laughter' is the joy of his parents' hearts; at last they have the substance to the covenantal promise that Abraham would

---

[16] Matthew 7: 14 (NKJV)
[17] Genesis 21: 5 (NKJV)

be the '*father of many nations*'[18]. And now, the Lord is asking him to sacrifice his son; to kill his only son whom he loves. Such is the measure of his faith and his willingness to sacrifice all for the Lord, that he obeys and leaves for the mountain the Lord would reveal.

How his heart must have been breaking at the thought of what he had to do, as he placed the wood in order, bound his son and laid him on the altar[19]. It was at the point of raising his knife to kill his son that the angel of the Lord called out from heaven and told him to stop, '*for now I know that you fear God, since you have not withheld your son, your only son from me*'[20]. A ram was caught in a nearby thicket, and Abraham took hold of the ram, killed it and offered it up as a burnt offering instead of his son. Incredible faith, but it is important to note that a sacrifice was still offered; an animal died on the altar.

There are so many more examples of sacrifice that we could mention, such as Hannah's offering and the vow she makes in 1 Samuel Chapters 1-2, and David's sacrifice in 2 Samuel 24. There are also the corporate animal sacrifices that were offered in Moses' tabernacle and the temple, including the national sacrifices made on the Holy Days, such as the Day of Atonement, when a male goat was sacrificed for the sins of the people[21]. And of course, the sacrifice of the Passover lamb, reminding the Jewish people of their rescue from Egypt[22].

---

[18] Genesis 17: 4 (NKJV)

[19] We do not know the age of Isaac at this point, but he is certainly old enough to carry the wood, v6, which suggests he could be a teenager or young man. Either way, with the strength to run away or overpower his father, he also chooses to walk in obedience and allow his father to bind him.

[20] Genesis 22: 12 (NKJV)

[21] Leviticus 16 (NKJV)

[22] Exodus 11-13 (NKJV)

But at the heart of all these sacrifices in the Old Testament, whether offered by individuals, tribes or nations, is the two-fold principle that firstly when God requires a sacrifice, He asks for the very best; and secondly, when we bring our offering, it has to cost us something. In 2 Samuel 24, when Araunah offered to donate the oxen for a burnt offering, and *'threshing implements and the yokes of the oxen for wood'*, David's reply to him was: *'No, but I will surely buy it from you for a price; nor will I offer burnt offerings to the Lord my God with that which costs me nothing'*[23]. David could have easily fallen for the temptation of accepting the gift, which would have covered all that was necessary for the sin offering. But he knew the difference between the fruit of his hands and the fruit of his heart. This offering had to cost him something.

> There was a price to be paid and it had to impact his life.

When Jesus died on the cross and His blood was poured out for us, He became the propitiation for our sin and for the whole world[24], so that no longer was the blood of an animal required to atone for our fallenness. He paid the price for us all[25]. His blood sacrifice on the cross became the final blood sacrifice required for sin, so that in dying and rising again He opened the way for us by faith to die with Him and rise with Him. This is why we are able to declare with confidence that if *'anyone is in Christ, he is a new creation; old things have passed away; behold all things have become new'*[26]. But in offering Himself for us, He did not bring an end to sacrifice. God does not change His law. Though the need for blood was fulfilled, the two-fold principle (as above) of God requiring a sacrifice and us bringing the best, and our offering having to cost us something, still continued into the early church and continues today. As Paul

---

[23] 2 Samuel 24: 24 (NKJV)
[24] 1 John 2: 2
[25] I Corinthians 6: 20; Ephesians 1: 7.
[26] 2 Corinthians 5: 14-17

writes to the church in Rome: *'I beseech you therefore, brethren, by the mercies of God, that you present your bodies a living sacrifice, holy, acceptable to God, which is your reasonable service'*[27]. Paul is referring to a 'living sacrifice' that costs us nothing less that our whole lives: our bodies, minds, hearts, strength, hopes, ambitions, choices and desires. This is the best that we can bring.

It is in view of this understanding of sacrifice that our 'sacrifice of praise' needs to be seen and realised. As the writer to the Hebrews expresses throughout his letter, and in this particular verse, it is only through Jesus, in Him, with Him and by Him that we could ever offer such a sacrifice of praise to God that is acceptable to Him. But the point is: not being dependant on our feelings, mood, circumstances, distractions, or even the storms we face in life, such a requirement for this sacrifice is simply that it is continually offered; it does not cease.

The question then is: how is such a continual sacrifice of praise possible?

The answer unassailably lies in our will and our willingness to offer to God the very best we have to give Him through it all; to offer Him the fruit of our lips, giving thanks to His name in the midst of the good and the bad alike.

> This is an act of our will and our daily willingness to praise Him.

Fruit, of course, is good for us. We know it is a good source of vitamins and minerals, and helps maintain our bodies for the long run. We know too that it does us little good to bite into an apple or take a segment of orange once in a while. Our daily intake is what really benefits our health. But good fruit has to grow on good trees and be rooted in good soil.

---

[27] Romans 12: 1 (NKJV)

The Greek word here for fruit, *karpos*, can literally mean fruit. But in the Scriptures, it is frequently used as a figure of speech to describe the fruitful outcome of our relationship with God and the things we do for Him; and this certainly seems to be the author's intention here. When we continually offer our sacrifice of praise there is a fruitful outcome in our relationship with God; the good fruit of praise delights the Father's heart[28]. When we daily give thanks to His name there is a benefit of abundance; our thanksgiving blesses the Lord[29]. But this fruitful outcome has to be sourced in the tree of life, the life of His presence, and be rooted in the good soil of His Word. David knew and understood this way of living and celebrates this with exuberance in Psalm 27 (NKJV).

> *The Lord is my light and my salvation; whom shall I fear?*
> *The Lord is the strength of my life; of whom shall I be afraid?*

He is declaring the truth of who God is and is celebrating the salvation and strength he has experienced in the face of his enemies and foes. These are not one-off attacks. The implication is that he has faced many dangers and threats, and yet his heart has not feared. Why? Because his confidence – his will and willingness to trust – has not wavered.

> *One thing I have desired of the Lord, that will I seek; that I may dwell in the house of the Lord all the days of my life, to behold the beauty of the Lord, and to inquire in His temple.*
> *For in the time of trouble, He shall hide me in His pavilion; in the secret place of His tabernacle He shall hide me; He shall set me high upon a rock.*

---

[28] Psalm 147: 11 (NKJV) and Psalm 149: 3-5 (NKJV)
[29] Psalm 103: 2 (NKJV)

He knows the only place to be is in the presence of God, whether he faces trouble or not. Day after day, there is a desire in his heart to behold God's beauty, and dwell with Him; there is a longing to be hidden in the secret place and to be set high upon the rock of His love and grace. This is the best place to be. And from this high place, knowing God is the one who exalts and lifts our heads above our enemies, David reveals the cycle of his life: namely, to continually rejoice and sing praise to the Lord.

> *Therefore I will offer sacrifices of joy in His tabernacle;*
> *I will sing, yes, I will sing praises to the Lord.*

This is the sacrifice of praise, the continual outward expression of our inner delight in the beauty and majesty of God's glory. This is the fruit of our lips, the ceaseless vocal celebration of that party in our hearts, knowing that no matter what God is our light and salvation and He delights in us, and we can always rejoice in Him.

The encouragement to us all is that such a sacrifice of praise is not prejudiced in any way; there is no special predisposition towards musical expertise or harmonious and tonal quality; this is not just for the choirs, orchestras and bands. The only requisite for continually offering our sacrifice of praise to God is our will and our willingness to do so. The words Moses spoke to his people could not be more befitting for us in this context:

> *'Whoever is of a willing heart, let him bring it as an offering to the Lord'*[30].

Our response should be like that of the people[31]. Through it all, we should come with hearts that are stirred and spirits that are willing, as each day we bring our sacrifice of praise to God the Father though

---

[30] Exodus 35: 5 (NKJV)
[31] Exodus 35: 21 (NKJV)

Jesus in the presence of His Holy Spirit, and continue to praise Him into glory, '… when we've no less days to sing God's praise than when we'd first begun'[32].

Personal response

1. Over the next week, read Psalm 27 (NKJV), and take time to meditate and listen to the Holy Spirit through this Psalm as you seek His presence and behold His beauty and glory. Be intentional about making diary appointments each day in the secret place, even if you can find only 10 minutes a day. If you have the desire for time with God, He will bless and increase the time you have with Him.
2. Ask the Holy Spirit to show you areas of your life where God may lose out on your praise, and your time with Him. Also ask Him to show you the fruit of your lips; namely, whether for example you criticize more than you praise, or speak negatively more than give thanks. If necessary, repent and make the conscious decision to begin each day with praise and thanksgiving.

Decree over your life:

I command my spirit to attention and my mind and body to come in line with my spirit, and I decree that through Jesus I will continually offer my sacrifice of praise to God, that is the fruit of my lips, giving thanks to His name.

---

[32] Words taken from the popular hymn, Amazing Grace, by John Newton, published 1779, although these words from the seventh verse by Anonymous/unknown, were published 1829.

The Silence of Praise

*The Lord is in His Holy temple,
Let all the earth keep silence before Him.
Habakkuk 2: 20 (NKJV)*

THERE ARE MOMENTS in life when we simply do not have the words to express our thoughts and feelings. I am not talking about being found out and having no more excuses left to give, or being caught in the act with nowhere to hide. I am specifically referring to those special occasions when the delight and wonder presented before us leaves us utterly speechless; those instances when our native language is simply too insufficient to capture the praise that is rising from deep within and we find ourselves being reduced to silence. Holding a newborn baby asleep in your arms, in awe of this beautiful miracle of life, is one such occasion that many would identify with. Amazed by the brilliance of an Impressionist painting or captivated by a panoramic view over a wonder such as the Grand Canyon or the Great Rift Valley, marveling at the beauty of woodland covered in a blanket of bluebells or delighting in the radiant shades of crimson and scarlet as the sun sets over the ocean would be other potential silencers. And it is not as if these glimpses of beauty are moments we can demand as a right or even recreate for our pleasure; rather than being found, they find you. They find you as you muddle along in the dark and stop to gaze up at the glorious starlight display above you and beyond. They find you as you shake off the rain from an unexpected downpour, and momentarily rest to delight in the vivid rainbow arched overhead. They find you as you stumble on a path you have walked all your life, pausing to marvel at a clump of wild orchids you have never noticed before.

For me, these moments seem to find me most often when I am high up in the mountains, by the seashore, or looking up at the night sky; stilled, astounded, amazed and in awe.

> Without question, creation has blessed us with so many opportunities for such wonder.

But there is another level to these aphonic moments that stop us in our tracks. There is a deeper and more profound suspension that leaves us speechless. These are the glimpses and the encounters with our Creator, the Holy One, where in the midst of His creative signs and wonders He chooses to reveal Himself in a new and fresh way.

For those with faith, as well as those without, God intentionally seeks us out and grabs our attention through 'beautiful collisions'[1], with His eternal desire of drawing us closer to Himself; such testimonies of this are as unique as they are life-changing. As we get to know God better – the Father, Son and Holy Spirit – we increasingly know His presence and power at work in our lives, and every touch from Him is as transforming as it is cathartic. Even our daily habits of praising Him, adoring Him, reading His word, and enjoying the Holy Spirit's peace and protection, is as wonderfully astounding as it is empowering. All of these times, individually and corporately, provide the opportunity for uninhibited and vociferous praise.

---

[1] This is a term I use to describe those key moments in our lives when it seems as if we have collided with God and felt His impact, and yet at the same time we have experienced the beauty of His love and grace. The near fatal car crash in Austria (which I describe in the introduction) is such an occasion for me.

Indeed, it is the most natural outward expression when we know whose image we are created in and how God loves to inhabit our praises, when we understand the reasons for praise and hunger to go deeper, and when we know the power of praise and how though all our experiences, good and bad, we continually offer up this sacrifice. As we have seen already, this is who we are: '*let everything that has breath praise the Lord*'[2].

But as contradictory as it may sound, and as paradoxical as it may appear in terms of our understanding of praise and praising, there is nonetheless a blip in the proceedings; an interruption to this rhythm of praise. What do I mean? I am talking about the unforeseen and unannounced experiences in the presence of God when the only response is to stand amazed with hearts burning, look with wonder as we perceive with delight, and bow with quiet adoration. I am referring to those brief periods of time when it seems as if everything we have learnt is insufficient and every word we possess is inadequate, and all we can do is '*be still and know that [He] is God*'[3]. In our busy and noisy lives such occurrences may not arise too frequently, but when they do we are entering into something very special.

The silence of praise!

The Bible has some unheralded examples of this that come to light only under closer inspection. For instance, when Moses experienced the glory of God in the cleft of the rock, in that moment '*he bowed his head toward the earth and worshipped*'[4] such was the splendour of standing on the rock with God covering him with His hand as He passed by[5]. We are told earlier in the chapter that the '*... Lord spoke*

---

[2] Psalm 150: 6 (NKJV)
[3] Psalm 46: 10 (NKJV)
[4] Exodus 34: 8 (NKJV)
[5] Exodus 33: 17-23 (NKJV)

to Moses face to face, as a man speaks to his friend[6], and later in the next chapter that *'the skin of his face shone while he talked with God'*[7] to such an extent that Aaron and the children of Israel were afraid to come near to him. But sandwiched between these descriptions of this special relationship with God we read of a remarkable and unique experience in which Moses' only response, however momentary (and we do not know the length of time), was to fall down in worship with his head bowed to the ground, speechless and in awe.

In Isaiah Chapter 6 we read of the prophet's inauguration into ministry. The first verse gives the date and the setting; the year is 740BC, when King Uzziah died after a long reign, and the location is the temple in Jerusalem. Here Isaiah has a vision of the Lord, the Holy One of Israel '... *sitting on a throne, high and lifted up, and the train of His robe filled the temple*'[8]. It was an earth-shaking, frightening and awe-inspiring visitation. He saw the Lord seated on His throne with the fiery angels, the seraphim, above; that in itself was enough for someone to sense their end might be near. He heard the multiple voices of these burning ones crying out to each other, proclaiming the holiness of God and making famous His glory throughout the whole earth[9]. He literally felt the doorposts of the temple shudder and move because of the power of *'the voice of Him who cried out'*[10], and was caught up in a smoking glory cloud that rises to fill the house. Not surprisingly his response was: *'woe is me, for I am undone'*, recognising his own and his people's uncleanness. We do not know how long it was before Isaiah spoke these words, but certainly this was an encounter that reduced him to silent praise for his '... *eyes [had] seen the King, the Lord of hosts*'[11]. He saw the

---

[6] Exodus 33: 11 (NKJV)
[7] Exodus 34: 29-30 (NKJV)
[8] Isaiah 6: 1 (NKJV)
[9] Cry, *qara*, also means to publish, proclaim, pronounce and make famous.
[10] Isaiah 6: 4 (NKJV)
[11] Isaiah 6: 5 (NKJV)

King of Kings! He looked upon the face of the Lord of Hosts, Jesus, whose '...*eyes [are] like a flame of fire* '[12]; such majesty, beauty, and holiness left him speechless for a time. Indeed this was a breathtaking moment in Isaiah's life, never to be forgotten, that set him on the path to being a voice for the nations.

In the New Testament, we equally find such moments of awe and wonder. When Jesus was transfigured on a high mountain, believed by some to be Mount Tabor[13], He had taken with him three of his disciples, Peter, John and James[14]. Imagining they were joining Jesus up the mountain to pray, as was often His custom, we are told in the gospel accounts that as He prayed the appearance of His face *'shone like the sun, and His clothes became white as the light. And behold Moses and Elijah appeared to them, talking with Him'*[15]. But it is the small additional detail that Luke shares which highlights this unheralded and unexpected moment of wonder. In verse 32, when Peter, John and James awoke from their sleep and were fully awake, Luke records that *'they saw His glory and the two men who stood with Him'* (NKJV). In the next verse, he mentions that it was only as Moses and Elijah departed that Peter spoke up. In other words, there was a period of time between the awakening and the departing, however brief, when these three unsuspecting friends could only gaze in awe at the true nature of Jesus, the One they had left all to follow. However momentary, they were caught up in the most majestic and beautiful presence of holiness, heaven overshadowing earth, with the saints on earth seeing the saints in paradise, and in their midst, beholding

---

[12] John's description of Jesus in Revelation 1: 14-15 (NKJV). Note Hebrews 13: 8: 'Jesus Christ is the same yesterday, today and forever' (NKJV).

[13] This is the traditional location. Mount Tabor lies at the eastern end of the Jezreel Valley, 11 miles (17 km) west of the Sea of Galilee, Israel. A Franciscan Church, the Church of the Transfiguration sits on top of the Mount.

[14] See the three gospel accounts: Matthew 17: 1-13 (NKJV); Mark 9: 1 – 13 (NKJV); Luke 9: 27 – 36 (NKJV).

[15] Matthew 17: 2-3 (NKJV)

the glory of Jesus. No wonder Peter eventually comes out with one of the biggest understatements in scripture: *'Master it is good for us to be here'*[16]. His suggestion of making three tents, and not knowing what he was saying, as Mark and Luke include, simply reveals the deep impact this experience was having on him and the others. And when the Father's voice came out of the cloud, they could only but fall on their faces in silent praise.

> This glorious, fearsome and awesome experience found them as they awoke from their sleep!

There are more examples to uncover in the gospel accounts. When Jesus appears through the solid walls of a locked household after His resurrection and says to the disciples: *'peace be with you'*, Luke and John include the moment. Initially there was fear and shock; they thought they were seeing a ghost. But when Jesus showed them His hands and His side, John records the disciples *'were glad when they saw the Lord'*[17]. They were joyful and filled with gladness. Speechless, they marveled at Jesus, who three days earlier they had witnessed die the most tortuous death on the cross, and now they even watched Him eat. A similar thing happened on the road to Emmaus when Jesus appeared to two disciples. As Luke records, Jesus comes along side them, talks with them, explains the scriptures and those things concerning Himself, and when they invite Him into their home and He broke the bread, and then vanished, their response was: *'Did not our hearts burn within us while He talked with us on the road'*[18]. In other words, praise was intensifying and reverberating in their hearts as they listened and stayed in His presence. Mary at the foot of Jesus and John falling at His feet as dead[19] are still more instances

---

[16] Luke 9: 33 (NKJV)
[17] John 20: 20 (NKJV). Also refer to Luke 24: 36-43 (NKJV). *Chairo* means to be glad, joyful and to rejoice.
[18] Luke 24: 32 (NKJV)
[19] Luke 10: 39 (NKJV) and Revelation 1: 17 (NKJV) respectively.

of such interruptions to this norm of praise; moments when our encounter with the Holy One is so glorious and captivating, that we are emptied of words but nonetheless filled with the praise ignited within us.

Even in heaven, we read of a moment when the praise of the angelic host is suspended and there is silence: *'When he opened the seventh seal, there was silence in heaven for about half an hour'*[20]. Admittedly there are a variety of opinions as to why there is silence and what the length of time signifies, and these views are not necessarily mutually exclusive. However, there is agreement in one key aspect; namely that up until this period, the heavenly praise has been a vociferous affair:

> *'You are worthy, O Lord, to receive glory and honour and power; for You created all things, and by Your will they exist and were created'*[21].

> *And they sang a new song, saying: 'You are worthy to take the scroll ... worthy is the Lamb who was slain to receive power and riches and wisdom, and strength and honour and glory and blessing'*[22].

Then comes this momentous interruption to these glorious songs of praise when the company of heaven is stilled before God and no sound is heard or uttered. At the very least – and the sense is that it is so much more than we could ever imagine – this can be seen as the right and befitting response to the Lamb, Jesus on the throne, who has opened the seventh seal. The pause in the proceedings may be within our time scale of about thirty minutes or it may be a

---

[20] Revelation 8: 1 (NKJV)
[21] Revelation 4: 11 (NKJV)
[22] Revelation 5: 9-14 (NKJV). See also Ch. 7: 10 -12 (NKJV).

greater or lesser period of time[23], but when the silence falls, it is out of a profound response of praise, adoration and worship, prior to the events which are about to happen.

>Heaven is stilled before the Lord.

What a beautiful and glorious representation of praise! In a world that succeeds in being masterful with noise and sounds – that which is welcome or not – such an interruption in heaven is certainly a mandate for earth. But when do we find earth stilled before the Lord?

By nature I am an extrovert and love to be around people, but there are occasions when I yearn for silence; my spirit, soul and body literally ache for peace and quiet. Even more so, I long for the stillness that comes from being in the presence of God, soaking in His love, and delighting in who He is and who I am to Him. When these special moments of glory and glimpses of God's majesty have found me unannounced, the silence of my praise has become such a powerful and intimate expression of my devotion and love for God. This may be something you can relate to!

However, this also raises the question: is there more that we can do to be found in such a place, speechless and in awe, silent and yet amazed? The Scriptures suggest there is.

In Zephaniah Chapter 1, the prophet encourages the people to *'be silent in the presence of the Lord God; for the day of the Lord is at hand'*[24]. He is exhorting God's people, in the face of the malignancy of their sin and the coming judgment day, to be intentional about hushing the noise of their idolatry and holding the tongue of their

---

[23] 2 Peter 3: 8: 'Beloved, do not forget this one thing, that with the Lord one day is as a thousand years, and a thousand years as one day' (NKJV).
[24] Zephaniah 1: 7 (NKJV)

sacrifices, and to be willfully still and silent before the face of God, knowing He alone is Lord. It is a cry for true praise as much as a call for heart-felt repentance: the two go together.

A similar message is found in Habakkuk Chapter 2. Again, in response to the stubbornness and hardheartedness of his countrymen, the prophet is repeatedly calling for repentance and is appealing to God's people to pursue silence before the Lord as an expression of praise: *'The Lord is in His Holy temple, let all the earth keep silence before Him'* (NKJV). *Hacah*, keeping silent, is all about intent; it is a choice and a purposeful act of adoration.

But as well as being intentional about refraining from making any kind of sound or noise before God, silence in the Scriptures can also mean 'waiting' and waiting can mean 'silence'. In Psalm 62, the opening words of David are: *'Truly my soul silently waits for God: from Him comes my salvation. He only is my rock and my salvation; He is my defense; I shall not be greatly moved'*[25]. The Hebrew word here for silently waiting, *duwmiyah*, is also used in Psalm 65, and it is here that we find a deeper illumination in relation to praise. At the beginning of the Psalm, David sings: *'Praise is awaiting You, O God, in Zion; and to You the vow shall be performed'*[26]. Defining the Hebrew word, *duwmiyah*, as 'awaiting', as most English Bible translations do, provides only part of its meaning; the 'silence' is missing. However, in an orthodox Jewish translation[27], the verse is worded as follows: *'To You, silence is praise, O God in Zion; and unto You shall the vow be fulfilled'*. This is deeply significant. This Hebrew text strongly implies that our praising is as much about our silence before God as about the sounds we lift up to His name; or to put it another way, our stillness before God can be as expressive

---

[25] Psalm 62:1 (NKJV)
[26] Psalm 65: 1 (NKJV)
[27] Psalm 65:1 (Stone Edition Tanach, by Rabbi Nosson Scherman, Artscroll.com)

as the songs we sing. In the Stone's edition, a commentary has been included as a footnote, written by one of the most renowned medieval French rabbinic scholars, Rashi (1044 – 1105), which explains this well:

> 'The praises of infinite God can never be exhausted. Silence is his most eloquent praise, since elaboration must leave glaring omissions'.

This is both an affirmation of our need to wait silently before God from time to time, but also the jubilation of the richness and magnitude of our praise when we do; an aspect that can so easily be overlooked in contemporary settings. King David is often extolled for his heart to celebrate the praises of God with singing and dancing, undignified and free; and that is right. However, he is not often given the credit for pursuing those times of stillness before God and those moments of 'eloquent' praise without words, where he simply waited on the Lord, quiet in His presence.

In the well known hymn 'Dear Lord and Father of mankind', written in 1872, the author John Greenleaf Whittier captures so well the habit of stillness and silence before the Father in the power of the Holy Spirit we see in the Gospel accounts which Jesus Himself modeled:

> O Sabbath rest by Galilee! O calm of hills above,
> where Jesus knelt to share with thee
> the silence of eternity
> interpreted by love!
> Interpreted by love![28]

---

[28] 'Dear Lord and Father of mankind', by John Greenleaf Whittier (1807 - 1892). It is interesting to note that Whittier, an American Quaker, disliked singing in church and strongly believed that God should be worshipped in silent meditation.

Jesus made the time and found the place for such moments of silence. As Luke writes: '*So He Himself often withdrew into the wilderness and prayed*'[29]; in other words, in His busy diary of events, this was a priority that often happened. Not only that, but He enjoyed these occasions alone: '*And when He had sent the multitudes away, He went up on the mountain by Himself to pray. Now when evening came, He was alone there*'[30]. It is worth noting that the Greek word for prayer in both these texts, *proseuchomai*, also means to worship.

Great and glorious moments of wonder find us in surprising ways, and so often they leave us speechless and still. These special faith-building interruptions cannot be anticipated or re-created, but nonetheless when they take place, they always draw us deeper into the silence of praise. However, as a number of these hidden Scriptural treasures reveal, this aspect of praise is something we can pursue with greater intent. Silence is not something to be feared; neither is it something to avoid. Our culture seems to work hard at keeping the noise levels up[31], and whilst this is the reality most of us face each day we do not need to be governed by it, especially when it comes to praise. If silence is praise, and praise is good for us, as we have already seen, then this is certainly something we should pursue more intentionally.

Of course there is a balance to maintain. Praise is the outward expression of an inner delight. It is the vocal celebration of a party in the heart, however big or small, momentary or continuous. God has created us to be a praising people, unashamed and free, to make

---

[29] Luke 5: 16 (NKJV)
[30] Matthew 14: 23 (NKJV)
[31] Not only do we contend with the constant noise of traffic, machinery, music played in shops etc., but technology allows us to be lost in our own world of sound, listening to music of our own choice, regardless of the noise that surrounds us. For example, a common description of a commuter would be someone wearing headphones.

noise and rejoice in Him with song and sound, and it is right that we should do so individually and corporately. This is how He has created us in His image and it is a beautiful and powerful thing. There is also power in our praising, and we can certainly never exhaust the opportunities and reasons for our praise.

However, in the midst of this truth and reality, the paradox of praise still remains that there needs to be a place for keeping still before God; it is a prerequisite of life that we create some space in our lives for growing deeper in our praising of Him with the sound of silence[32]. Sometimes God will arrive unannounced and find us with a touch of His glory, and these interruptions to the norm will be moments to cherish as we stand in silence, in awe of who He is. But at other times, He desires to be found by us in these intimate and silent moments as we seek Him. They can be just as glorious and profound, but require the intent of our hearts for such an encounter. They require the pursuit of hushing the noise around us, and the practice of creating time to know God better in the stillness. When we find such time, suspend our requests, wait on Him with burning hearts, and bow with quiet adoration, we will discover more and more the wonder of His majesty, the beauty of His holiness, and the glory of His nature as we rest in the silence of His praise.

Personal response

1. Over the next week, find a location that brings you peace and joy, and make time simply to be quiet before God. In the silence, allow your praise to rise up to Him, and enjoy being in His presence. No lists or agendas.

---

[32] The author is aware that a key part of being still before God is listening to His voice. Whilst this is essential in our walk with the Lord, this is not the focus in this book; the silence and stillness here is in the context of praise.

2. Ask the Holy Spirit to reveal your relationship to silence, especially when it comes to being with Him. If necessary, repent, and ask the Holy Spirit to help you learn what it is to gaze in wonder, stand amazed, bow in adoration, and sit at His feet.

Decree over your life:

I command my spirit to attention and my mind and body to come in line with my spirit, and I decree: I will be intentional about creating times in my life to be still in presence of God, and to discover more of the wonder of His majesty, the beauty of His holiness, and the glory of His nature as I rest in the silence of His praise.

To Live is Praise

I will bless the Lord at all times;
His praise shall continually be in my mouth.
My soul shall make its boast in the Lord;
The humble shall hear of it and be glad.
Oh magnify the Lord with me
And let us exalt His name together
Psalm 34: 1-3 (NKJV)

IN NOVEMBER 2014 I had the privilege of travelling with a group of church leaders to China. We spent some time in Shanghai and then Nanjing, before flying south to the Kunming province to meet with Christian believers and distribute Bibles. On one occasion, we visited a Miao ethnic village high up in the mountains in the Lufeng County, called Bajiao, (translated 'Banana'). The journey there took us five hours by minibus, before being transported in primitive wooden carts up the steep mountain pass to the village. Along with the precarious yet hilarious convoy to the top, the greeting we received will certainly stay with me for a very long time to come. We were the first British people this village had ever encountered, and far from approaching us with suspicion, they welcomed us with the most beautiful songs of praise; and the singing did not cease. They sang as we entered their church; they sang during the service and after we handed out Bibles; and they sang to us as we left. We were told afterwards that this Miao tribe is known among the locals as the 'singing farmers'. What a reputation to have! Praise was so deeply embedded into every part of their daily lives, from singing as they worked in the fields to celebrating as they welcomed strangers into their midst, it literally shined (*halal*) out of them like the sun!

What an impact the church would have today if its fame and renown centred on unceasing *halal* praise? This is how we are made in the image of our praising Creator, and this is how we are created to live. As David proclaims, even when his life was in danger and he had to feign madness in order to escape[1]:

I will bless the Lord at all times; His praise shall continually be in my mouth[2].

David is not re-inventing a new way of life; neither is he implying a departure from an old pattern to a new model of being. He is simply professing an existential condition that he knows has to involve each moment of every day. 'At all times' (*eth*) means always; 'continually' (*tamiyd*) from its root, means to stretch, as in an indefinite extension; in other words, to extend in all ways. They are words that describe not only the continuation of being but also the constancy of doing; namely, to be a people of praise, like the Miao tribe, who bless the Lord and celebrate His goodness day and night in every season, year after year and through it all. This was Paul's exhortation when he writes to the church in Philippi and says: '*rejoice in the Lord always. Again, I will say rejoice*'[3]. The message is clear in both Old and New Testaments:

> Always praise! Praise in all ways!

But such a mandate requires further qualification in order to become a commission that we can fully embrace into the future and a mission

---

[1] I Samuel 21: 10-15 (NKJV)
[2] Psalm 34: 1 (NKJV)
[3] Philippians 4: 4 (NKJV)

that we can wholeheartedly live out each day. Otherwise it could easily become another pulpit-fuelled charge that sounds admirable from a distance but unattainable closer to home.

In Isaiah Chapter 54 we discover such a qualification. Whether it is read in its original setting or applied for our day, this is a prophetic word depicting the glorious future that God promises to His people, and continues to promise us today. But in the midst of the envisioned covenant of peace, prosperity and protection there is a powerful exhortation that can be applied in the context of perpetual praise. The prophet begins by saying: *'sing O barren! Break forth into singing, and cry aloud...'* (NKJV). In other words, there is a call to rejoice with a voice of triumph and an invitation to sing aloud, even in the midst of barrenness[4]. But then comes the qualifier:

> *'Enlarge the place of your tent, and let them stretch out the curtains of your dwellings; do not spare; lengthen the cords, and strengthen your stakes. For you shall expand to the right and to the left, and your descendants will inherit the nations, and make the desolate cities inhabited'*[5].

The verbs that are used here all speak of expansion and magnification: 'enlarge' (*rahab*) means to be wider and broader, and to increase the state of spatial dimension to allow room to move and grow; it can also mean to boast[6]; 'stretch out' (*natah*) has the notion

---

[4] For example, *Ranan*, sing, literally means a ringing cry, or a twang of a bowstring, but when applied to praise, means to sing aloud with a voice of triumph, and greatly rejoice. Also refer back to the chapter on the Sacrifice of Praise.

[5] Isaiah 54: 2-3 (NKJV)

[6] For example, in 1 Samuel 2: 1, Hannah prays: 'My heart rejoices in the LORD; in the LORD my horn is lifted high. My mouth boasts over my enemies,

of spreading out and covering an even larger area extending from the source; 'do not spare' (*chasak*) means do not restrain, reserve or withhold anything; 'lengthen' (*arak*) means to make longer, draw out, prolong and outlive; and 'strengthen' (*chazak*) implies a higher degree of intensity; it also means to squeeze.

> There is a realisation of expansion and increase in every direction that intrinsically applies to the whole area of praise and praising[7].

Here we have a compelling insight into the nature of our being; namely, a revelation of God's heart for us to be ever expanding in our continual praise of Him, both reflecting our Creator God who is forever stretching out His praise over us, but also fulfilling an innate potential in us, made in His image, to magnify His name[8]. In other words, having been created for praise and knowing the reasons, depths, power and sacrifice of praise as God inhabits the realm of our praises, there is an immanent and connatural propensity in us to be able to offer more: to 'enlarge' the room we make for praise and keep on enlarging the place of praise in our lives; to expand the time we give for praise and keep on expanding each moment with God in His presence; and to 'magnify' the creative expressions of our praise, and to continually increase the depth and breadth in all we do.

> In the backdrop of 'always praise' there is 'always more'!

---

for I delight in your deliverance'. (NIV)

[7] The author is fully aware that this passage can and has been applied in many different contexts. However, it is his firm belief that verse 1 sets the foundation for expounding verses 2 and 3 in the framework of praise, and at the very least (along with other interpretations) can be understood in this way.

[8] '*Oh magnify the Lord with me*', Psalm 34: 3 (NKJV). 'Magnify', *gadal*, means to increase, make bigger, to keep on advancing.

But such an expansion has to be intentional and enduring. It cannot be casual or short-lived. The reality is that God knows perfectly the implications when it is the latter. He knows for example what happens when our voice of praise is *chasak* (sparing); the sound is feeble and impoverished to those around us. He knows the effect on our gatherings when our approach is restrained; a trickle of rejoicing and joy barely reaches the front door. And He knows the ramifications for the wider community when we hold back in our praising; the world passes by unchanged and unmoved. This is of course the antithesis of how we are created to be, as we have seen throughout this book. Just as muscles atrophy when they are not used, so does our voice and creativity waste away when it is restrained and enervated. The point is: nothing remains the same! We shrink or we grow in our desire to praise; we constrict or we expand in our offering of praise. But for there to be expansion we have to keep moving towards the 'more'.

Conversely God knows what happens when we increase our capacity to praise, because He is inextricably involved with us. He knows the atmosphere around us is transformed when we 'stretch out' and magnify His name with greater intensity and passion, because He has created us for this very purpose and delights in us when we give Him our all and then more. And whilst the logic might seem paradoxical, the reality is consistent with who we are; there is always a newer song to sing and a greater offering to bring:

> '*Oh sing to the Lord a new song! Sing to the Lord all the earth. Sing to the Lord, bless His name. Proclaim the good news of His salvation from day to day. Declare His glory among the nations, His wonders among all peoples. For the Lord is great and greatly to be praised*'[9].

---

[9] Psalm 96:1-4a (NKJV)

The Psalmist has such a vision of expansion and magnification. He is filling the imagination with the possibility of both continual increase in that which is new, when it comes to our songs of praise, but also that which is transforming, when it comes to its power among the nations. The message is:

> Sing and keep singing and people will stop and notice. Declare and keep declaring and the nations will take heed, for the Lord is great and is the greatest to be praised.

Surely this is what our world needs to see and encounter today? The church on the 'magnification trail' when it comes to praise! Indeed, this is what the prophet Isaiah envisioned in Chapter 54. As we enlarge, expand and extend the offering of our praise, God, who is faithful to His promises, will not only bring life and fruitfulness to areas that are dry and barren, but will bring blessing to our descendants and the nations they inherit[10]. It is as if the prophet is shouting from the rooftops: make more room for praise in your life and see what God will do.

> Enlarge the room for praise.

Making room for praise is so important. Anyone living in tight quarters knows how difficult it is to be expressive when there is little room to breathe. Those living in the slums we have visited in Kenya experience this day after day, existing in one room with up to ten family members. Without exception, no one there who I have talked to would dwell in such conditions by choice. Why then do we so easily choose this condition when it comes to our praise? As we have seen already, too often the space for praise is squashed and restricted, when we should be yearning for greater room.

---

[10] Isaiah 54: 3 (NKJV)

In many of the Psalms we see such a yearning. For example, in Psalm 24, the Psalmist David celebrates the King and His kingdom, and acknowledges who it is who can seek the Lord and *'seek [His] face'*[11]. He then includes a musical notation, *'selah'*[12], that is often overlooked but is of paramount importance. Admittedly there is some discrepancy about its actual meaning. The word *'selah'* could be derived from two Hebrew words meaning to 'exalt' and to 'lift up'[13]. Certain commentators relate it to the word, *'calah'*, meaning to 'weigh up' or to 'value'. The word itself can be translated to mean 'pause', in terms of taking an interlude in performing a Psalm, or having an intermission from either the voices or instruments. In actual fact, whether it means one or all of these descriptions – value, exalt and lift up, or pause - there is a powerful interplay at work; namely, it creates the room and values the space for spontaneous and extemporary praise. In other words, *'selah'* gives permission for 'more' than is planned, and 'more' than is rehearsed. We need more *'selah'* moments in our gatherings and in our life of praise. We need to enlarge the room we make for praising, whether we are gathered together in our church meetings, celebrating God's love and faithfulness, or on our own breaking out in spontaneous exaltation. Whatever flows for us individually and corporately, we have to be intentional and enduring about making more room for praise in our lives. It will not just happen! But alongside the enlarging of the space we make for praise sits the expansion of time we give for praise in our lives.

Expand the time for praise.

At one level it is a strange concept to imagine we can expand or stretch time. Time of course is a precious commodity! Twenty-four hours often seem too short to achieve the long list of things we have

---

[11] Psalm 24: 6 (NKJV)

[12] This word is mentioned seventy-four times in the Hebrew text; seventy-one times in the Psalms and three times in Habakkuk Chapter 3.

[13] s_lah, "to exalt, praise"; and s_lal, "to lift up."

planned for the day; and common to many people, especially in Western culture, is the reality that we are always pushed for time. Our busy lives are not conducive to creating time for praise and prayer. But when we give our time to God He always makes more of it than we can imagine; and when we keep giving more, we are never in debt. Such a statement is not wishful thinking; neither is it naïve to the time restraints and pressures on our lives. It is rooted in Scripture and discovered through experience.

For many years now I have been working more than sixty hours a week, but I have also been expanding the time I spend with God as I have pursued a life of continual praise with greater desire and discipline. In the course of this journey, I have also discovered that God longs to expand His time with me. Why should I be surprised? From the beginning, God has treasured His time with us in the outlining of the Sabbath principle of rest[14]. But there is more to this pearl of great price.

In Psalm 84, the Psalmist reveals a deeper reality. In the context of celebrating the loveliness of God's presence and the longing of his heart and flesh 'for the living God', the author pens what is really on his heart: *'For a day in Your courts is better than a thousand'*[15]. In other words, time spent with the Lord of hosts is far greater than a multiple of a thousand expended elsewhere. I love the Passion translation of this verse:

> *'For just one day of intimacy with You is like a thousand days of joy rolled into one'*[16].

---

[14] See Genesis 2: 1-3 (NKJV), Exodus 20: 8-11, and 31: 12-18 (NKJV).
[15] Psalm 84: 10 (NKJV). Even though the title refers to this being a Psalm of the sons of Korah, a number of commentators, such as Matthew Henry, believe it has the hallmark of David, and was written when he was forced by Absalom's rebellion to leave his beloved city; they compare it with Psalm 63 (NKJV).
[16] The Psalms: Poetry on Fire, The Passion Translation, 2nd Edition, translated from the Greek and Aramaic Texts by Dr. Brian Simmons, 5 Fold Media, LLC, 2014, page 166.

The writer then goes on to say: *'For the Lord God is a sun and shield; the Lord will give grace and glory; no good thing will He withhold from those who walk uprightly'*[17]. Along with his desire for expanded time in God presence is the intimate knowledge that God withholds no good thing, including His time with us. The Hebrew word for withhold, *mana*, also means to keep back, refrain and restrain. When we are in the courts of the Lord, God does the very opposite of restraint; when we seek Him out in the secret place He withholds nothing including the parameters of time; He stretches this tent! Whether it was through revelation, experience or both, the author of this Psalm certainly reveals the route by which we can know and enjoy this expanded time with the Lord. And after all, if the Lord can make the sun stand still, as Joshua and the Israelites experienced[18], and *'one day is as a thousand years and a thousand years is like a day'*[19], as the Apostle Peter writes, He is able to expand and lengthen the cords of time we spend with Him, however mysterious this may seem. All things are possible with God[20].

By way of encouragement, I can personally testify that this is true. Increasingly I am finding that times I spend with the Lord in praise and adoration, though the clock affirms a certain time period, the reality of the experience reveals such a longer and greater encounter, where minutes can literally seem like hours; and I am less surprised when this happens. If the Lord of time and eternity is able to expand (or restrict) time, He is certainly able to bless us in such a way when we enter into His courts with hearts filled with praise. But the key to expanding our time with Him is to long for His presence.

---

[17] Psalm 84: 11 (NKJV)
[18] Joshua 10: 12-15 (NKJV)
[19] 2 Peter 3: 8 (NKJV)
[20] Matthew 19: 26 (NKJV)

Magnify the creativity of praise

We are living in such exciting times when it comes to creative expressions. Not only are the resources to hand so much more useable, available and varied, but the culture we are a part of continually stretches out to celebrate the new, the bold, the beautiful, the exemplary, the exquisite and the exceptional. Of course, our Creator God, who forever excels in His creativity, has made us to be like Him and all creativity is sourced in Him. So, there is always room for extending our creative expressions in praise, and pursuing an excellence in this offering to God both in our churches as well as within our communities. Creativity is not just about music as some imagine. Dance, prophetic art, poetry, lighting and visuals all play an important part to our praise and praising, and this is certainly something that continually needs exploring and developing in terms of increasing the depth and breadth of what we bring. However, our music and the songs of praise we sing are key to this magnification. In many ways the inscription in the organ loft of Whitfield's Tabernacle[21] summarise this creative expression so well:

> *Make a large place in your life for music and it will bring you a priceless reward. All the desires of your heart will come closer to you as you become attuned to the rhythm and harmony of music. In the hour of rest, music will uplift your spirit and give refreshment to every faculty of your being. In the hour of work, you will rejoice in the strength and energy that music will bring. In the hour of prayer, music will quicken the aspirations of your soul.*

---

[21] Whitefield's Tabernacle on Tottenham Court Road, a church in London, England, also called Tottenham Court Road Chapel, was destroyed on Palm Sunday, 25th March 1945, by the last V-2 rocket to fall on London in the Second World War.

> *In the hour of fellowship, music will blend your spirit with others in unity and understanding.*

Where do we do go from here?

Throughout the process of this book, we have seen how our praising Creator God has made us a people of praise, and loves to inhabit our praises. We have shown how easily we lose the reason for praise, but in every moment, there are a myriad of reasons to praise our Lord and Saviour. Too often we are restrained in our praising by familiarity and restraint, but God loves it when we dive into the depths of the freedom He has created for us, as the deep in Him calls to the deep in us, knowing there is greater power to heal, comfort, save and protect when we approach Him with child-like perfected praise. We have revealed the importance of offering our sacrifice of praise continually, through all the experiences of life, and that there are momentous interruptions when we are caught up in the silence of praise. Finally, we have acknowledged the mandate to praise at all times, in all ways, knowing there is always more.

> This is what the Bible teaches and this is how God has purposed us to live, move and have our being[22];
> to live is praise.

But we have to make a response! We have to choose this beautiful and powerful essence of life for ourselves. In truth, if the end result of you reading this book is to set it aside or shelve it without there being any change to your pattern of praise, then the intention in writing this work has been lost on you. This was never meant to be a theological exposition with a collection of personal stories. The only meaningful outcome for the author is for you to know your true identity as God has created you to be, and to pursue a life of praise

---

[22] Acts 17:28 (NKJV)

and praising day after day, joining with creation's choir in heaven and earth. This was George Herbert's exhortation, expressed in his much-loved poem: 'let all the world in every corner sing, my God and King'[23].

Coming back to the apple tree and the experience that began this journey of praise for me back in the summer of 1984, I have learnt to realise that there is no limit to the literal and figurative apple trees that we can stand under, immersed in the presence of God, as we lift up our praise to the One who is worthy of it all. In fact I have come to discover that such a covering and immersion can take place wherever we are and whatever is going on in our lives, and is far greater, higher, deeper and wider than we can know or understand.

The local pastors in the Kunming area of Southern China have a proverb that says: 'You can tell how many seeds are in an apple, but you can not tell how many apples are in a seed'. This is certainly true with our praise. When our praise is sown as a seed into the realm of God's presence, our praising is far greater than the sum of its parts, and its transforming power spreads out and extends beyond anything we can imagine. This is our praising God who transforms the atmosphere when we live a life of praise in Him and for Him.

If this is new to you, then with the Holy Spirit's help, find a figurative apple tree as a starting point, stand under it, and let Him reveal anew His wonderful presence as you exalt Him with your praising. If you are experienced and well versed in songs of praise then, with the Holy Spirit's help, find a figurative apple tree in the midst of normality, stand under it, and let Him reveal afresh His wonderful presence as you magnify Him with your praising. But wherever you stand and whoever you stand with, immerse yourself in the rivers of

---

[23] George Herbert 1593-1633: The Poetical Works Of George Herbert, ed. George Gilfillan. Edinburgh: James Nichol, 1853.

living waters[24], knowing there is so much more of God's great love and grace for you, as you make this decree over your life:

> I command my spirit to attention and my mind and body to come in line with my spirit and I decree: *'I will live to praise you, O Lord my God, with all my heart, mind, soul and strength, and I will live to glorify Your name forever and a day'.*

---

[24] John 7: 37 (NKJV)

Appendix

The following poems and songs are a collection that has been written over a number of years as an expression of living a life of praise. It is the author's intention that they draw the reader into the realms of deeper praise, but also inspire the reader in the creation of new songs of praise

If the reader chooses to use the lyrics of one or more of these songs or poems in public or for the purpose of recording, please acknowledge the author in a way that is both godly and legal, and be blessed as you seek your own special apple tree under which you find the sweet presence of God in the secret place.

> *'Oh, sing to the Lord a new song!*
> *Sing to the Lord all the earth.*
> *Sing to the Lord, bless His name;*
> *Proclaim the good news of His*
> *Salvation from day to day.*
> *Declare His glory among the nations,*
> *His wonders among all peoples.*
> *For the Lord is great and greatly to be praised'.*
> *Psalm 96:1-4 (NKJV)*

You are holy

Lord I worship you in the stillness of my heart,
As I come before your throne to worship you.
I bow down in adoration
And acknowledge your perfection
And cry 'Holy, holy is your name'.

You are holy, you are holy!
Lord God Almighty!
You are holy, you are holy,
And I worship you.

August 1984

The Love of God means Calvary

The love of God means Calvary
Nothing less that this;
The breaking of His heart for me
To bear my sinfulness
The laying down of majesty
The miracle of grace
The love of God means Calvary
Nothing less that this.

Like a stream that's overflowing,
A river rushing to the sea,
So my heart wells up with thankfulness
For all you've done for me.
Like a light in the darkness,
A beacon shining in the night,
So my hope is in You alone,

And in this certainty.

The love of God means Calvary
Nothing less than this.

September 1997

The fragrance fills the air

She looked not to the head
But to the feet of her Lord.
She cared not for the cost,
But gave to the One she adored.
Tears on her face
As the fragrance filled that place.
The Lord knew the heart
Of what she had done.
It was a simple act of love
That affected everyone.

Some criticised the waste,
Others silently agreed.
It was not worth the cost,
When the poor were still in need.
Tears on her face
As the fragrance filled the place.
The Lord fought for the heart
Of what she had done.
It was a simple act of love
That challenged everyone.

What is the cost of my devotion?
What's in my heart to show I care?

Do I take cheap perfume to anoint Him?
Or is it everything I have,
And the fragrance fills the air.

This simple act of love to the Anointed One.

October 1997

Jesus, you are faithful

You desire from me the offering of worship
You rejoice to see the praises on my lips
You delight to be my shelter
And the rock of my salvation
Lord of all, you are faithful to me
Lord of all, you are faithful to me.

Jesus, you are faithful
Jesus, you are gracious,
Jesus, you are everything to me.

Jesus, you are faithful
Jesus, you are gracious,
Jesus, you are everything to me,
everything.

September 2004

With your glory

Father, Father, we're resting in your steadfast love
Jesus, Jesus, we're dwelling in your saving love
Spirit, Spirit, we're breathing in your healing love.

Let your glory fall
Let your light shine down
Radiate our hearts with your fire
Let Your fresh wind blow
Let Your river flow
Saturate our lives with your glory,
with your glory.

With your glory, our eyes can see you
With your glory, our hearts can know you
With your glory our face burns for you
With your glory, and all for You.

October 2007

Come to us
(based on Hosea 6)

As surely as the rising sun, as certain as its light
You will come to those who seek you, You will come.
As surely as the winter rains, as certain as the spring
You will come to those who seek you, You will come.
We wait in expectation,
we bow in adoration,
we acknowledge you are Lord of all,
and we're living to know you more.

Come to us, abide in us
Our Lord Emmanuel
Stir our hearts, ignite our lives
Our Lord Emmanuel,
Emmanuel, God with us
We're living to know you more.

As surely as Your Sovereignty, as certain as Your love
You will come to those who seek you, You will come.
As surely as Your faithfulness, as certain as Your grace
You will come to those who seek you, You will come.
We wait in expectation,
we bow in adoration,
we acknowledge you are Lord of all
and we're living to know you more.

Jesus, light of the world,
come and live in us.

November 2007

What a friend I have in Jesus

What a friend I have in Jesus
What a friend I have in you
You are always there besides me
What a friend I have in you, Jesus

You are faithful, You are loving
You are steadfast, You are good
You are beautiful to me
You are wonderful to be with
You are everything a perfect friend can be
What a friend, what a friend you are

You are gracious, You are caring
You are giving, You are strong
You are passionate for me
You are glorious to be with

You are everything a perfect friend can be
What a friend, what a friend, you are.

No greater love has anyone than your love on the cross
You gave your life for everyone so that none would be lost
You no longer call us servants but you call us your friends,
What a friend I have in Jesus, what a friend, you are.

November 2009

We come to drink
(based on John 7: 37)

We are thirsty for the purity of your presence
We are thirsty for the stillness of your peace
We are thirsty for the flow of your mighty power
So we come to you,
In faith we come to drink.

We are thirsty for the beauty of Your Holiness
We are thirsty for the freshness of your love
We are thirsty for the streams of living water
So we come to you,
In faith we come to drink.

We come to drink,
Drink of your Holy Presence
We come to drink,
Drink of your love and mercy
We long for streams of living water
and torrents of your grace
To flood our hearts,

and cover everything in us.
We are thirsty for you,
We are thirsty for you, Jesus.

March 2010

Completely
(based on Psalm 139)

If I run away, you are there, you are there;
If I turn astray, you are there.
You are there, if I rise on the wings of the dawn;
You are there, if I sail to the far side of the sea.

If I hide my face, you are there, you are there;
If I lose my faith, you are there.
You are there, if I climb high to the heavens above;
You are there, if I fall down to the depths of the earth

You search me,
you know my ways,
when I sit and rise;
You see my thoughts from afar.
You lead me,
you hold me tight,
you're by my side
I know you love me completely

How precious are your thoughts
Too marvelous for me
I know that I am yours
completely.

February 2011

I am created to know you

I am created to know you,
and be known by you,
God of grace.
I am created to love you,
and be loved by you,
God of love.
I am created to walk
with you in Paradise
I choose to live each day for you,
and I choose to live the way
that you have made me.

God of grace,
God of love,
God creator and redeemer
In you I live,
in you I move,
In you I have my being.
I live to glorify you
exalt and magnify you,
and worship you forever.

May 2011

Deep calls out to deep
(based on Psalm 42)

Where can I find hope?
Without you, there's no anchor for my soul.
Where can I find peace?
Without you, there's no shelter from the storm.

Where can I find love?
Without you, there's no power as strong as death.

Deep calls out to deep
In the roar of your waterfalls.
My soul cries out to you.
All your waves go over me
In the night your song is with me
I will say: you are my rock!
Jesus, I will hope in you.
Deep calls out to deep
In the roar of your waterfalls.
My soul cries out to you.

May 2011

Wake up

Wake up, rise up and sing songs of jubilee.
Shake up, break out and fling wide the gates of glory.
Take up, step out and ring bells of liberty.
Wake up, rise up and sing to the King.

We are children of destiny
A generation who knows the Father's love
We have passion for purity
With every step we will set the world on fire.

Wake up, rise up and sing songs of jubilee.
Shake up, break out and fling wide the gates of glory.
Take up, step out and ring bells of liberty.
Wake up, rise up and sing to the King.

We are makers of history
A holy nation who knows the Father's power
We have passion for jubilee
With all out heart we will set the world on fire.

We are more than conquerors
Lovers of the King of glory
We are mighty warriors
Burning with His love.
Every stronghold crumbles
Powers of darkness flee
In the name of Jesus
It is jubilee.

February 2012

Beautiful Saviour
(Adored by you)

Beautiful Saviour,
Beautiful Lord
The way you have loved me
I know I'm adored
You reach out your arms
And extend your embrace
You gaze through the storms
And search for my face
To show me your smile
Reveal your love
And tell me
again and again
I'm adored by you.

September 2012

To the One who saves

There's a knock on the door and a voice that says: be open.
There's a light in the storm and a sound that calls: be still.
There's a breath in the air and a whisper heard: come nearer
To the One who saves.

There is sight for the blind in the voice that says: be open.
There is strength for the weak in the sound that calls: be still.
There is love for the lost in the whisper heard: come nearer
To the One who saves.

You are the voice of salvation
You are the light of the world.
You are the hope of the nations,
Jesus, You are the One who saves.

I come to you,
to the One who saves;
I come to you,
Jesus.

December 2012

King of glory
(based on Psalm 24)

Who may ascend the hill of the Lord?
Who may stand in Your presence?
Those with clean hands and a pure heart
and a soul surrendered to you.

Blessing and honour and righteousness
belong to those who seek your face.
God, we lift up our heads and open our hearts;
let your glory come.

King of glory, strong and mighty
King of Glory enter in
Lord of heaven, pure and holy
Let your glory enter in this place.

The earth is the Lord's
and all that is within it!
The earth is the Lord's
and His fullness dwells within it.

February 2013

Beautiful

Beautiful is your nature
Beautiful is your name
Beautiful is your character
Beautiful is your way
There's no one, no one like You;
There's no one as beautiful as you.

Beautiful are you Jesus
Beautiful are your eyes
Beautiful are your gazes
Beautiful are your smiles
There's no one, no one like You;
There's no one as beautiful as you.

Oh the beauty of your holiness
Oh the wonder of your love
Oh the glory of your majesty
There's no one as beautiful as You;
There's no one as beautiful as You.

Jesus, Jesus
Jesus, Jesus
There's no one, no one like you;
There's no one as beautiful as You.

March 2013

You are near

You are near when lives are torn apart
You are near when loss comes at the start
You are near to every broken heart
You are near

You are near calming the fiercest storm
You are near raising us when we fall
You are near loving us through it all
You are near

Near to us, saving us,
reviving us with Holy fire
You are, Jesus, you are;
Holding us, healing us,
loving us with everything
You are, Jesus, you are.

We give you all our worship
We give you all the honour
Jesus, we give you all our praise.
Near us, Jesus,
Nearer we come to you.

September 2013

Come as the light

We can do no-thing without you Lord
We can be no lamp without your light in us.

Come as the light that shines in the darkness
Come as the fire that burns in our hearts
Come as the wind that blows every storm away
Come Holy Spirit and fall on us.

We can break no chains without you Lord
We can bear no fruit without your life in us.

Come as the light that shines in the darkness
Come as the fire that burns in our hearts
Come as the wind that blows every storm away
Come Holy Spirit and fall on us.

We will shine like the stars in the darkness
We will fan your burning flame
We will move with the wind of your presence
For the glory of Your name.

April 2016

You are good and you do good
(based on Psalm 119:68)

Your word is better to me
Than a thousand coins of silver and gold
Your way is greater than all the wisdom of man
I desire to know you more.

You are good, and You do good
Lord, teach us the goodness of your ways
You are good and you do good
We delight in the goodness of Your grace.

Your mercy scatters the darkness
Your kindness cracks the ice
Your love moves every mountain
And forever your goodness shines.

October 2016

Great are you Lord
(based on Psalm 96)

Beneath the deepest depths
Above the highest heights
Before the first born breath
Beyond the furthest lights
Your praise rings out
Your glory shines
The beauty of Your holiness resounds.

All through the darkness night
Amidst the raging storm

Along the narrow path
Until the light of dawn
Your praise rings out
Your glory shines
The splendour of Your majesty resounds.

Great are you Lord
And greatly to be praised;
Great are You Lord
The name above all names.
Great are You Lord
All honour, power and majesty are Yours
And Yours alone
Great are You Lord.

Your name, Your reign,
Your grace, Your ways
Your love, Your life,
You are worthy of all praise

August 2017

About the Author

Phil Warren is married to Heather and has two daughters. His passion is to see people revived, restored and fired up to have a burning heart for worship and a radiant heart for the lost. He is an Anglican Minister and leads two vibrant and growing churches in Jersey, Channel Islands. He is also a Director of Catch the Fire UK and a Director of the Kenyan Children's Project.

Lightning Source UK Ltd.
Milton Keynes UK
UKHW03f1810030418
320464UK00001B/49/P